THE LAW AND PHILOSOPHY OF WAR

A Very Brief Introduction for Everyone
– tutti fratelli

JOSEPH EDWARDS

Cara Press • 2025

THE LAW AND PHILOSOPHY OF WAR
A Very Brief Introduction for Everyone
– tutti fratelli

JOSEPH EDWARDS
Published by Cara Press

Printed Worldwide
First Printing 2025
First Edition 2025

10 9 8 7 6 5 4 3 2 1

ISBN: 978-0-9836530-6-6

Interior Book Design by Walt's Book Design
www.waltsbookdesign.com

THE LAW AND PHILOSOPHY OF WAR

DEDICATION

To all those warriors who have heard that distant, faint whisper with the ears of their heart and have made the right choice

Epigraph

"Even war has its laws."

— Cicero

TABLE OF CONTENTS

Preface 1
Introduction 5
Why the Law of War Matters 5
Chapter 1 15
The Historical Roots of Restraint 15
Chapter 2 31
Defining the Law of War, Part 1: Vocabulary and Purpose 31
Defining the Law of War, Part 2: Sources of Authority 37
Defining the Law of War, Part 3: Core Principles 43
Part 4: Combatants and Non-Combatants 47
Part 5: Perfidy and Quarter 52
Part 6: Necessity, Proportionality, and Humanity 55
Chapter 3 63
The Sources of Authority (Part 1: Treaties and Conventions) 63
(Part 2) 67
(Part 3) 73
Chapter 4 81
From Catastrophe to Law (Part 1) 81
(Part 2) 85
Chapter 5 91
The Conduct of Hostilities (Part 1) 91
(Part 2) 95
Chapter 6 101
Weapons: What Can and Cannot Be Used (Part 1) 101
(Part 2) 109
Chapter 7 115
Prisoners of War (Part 1) 115
Prisoners of War (Part 2) 122
Prisoners of War (Part 3) 129
Chapter 8 137
Occupation Law (Part 1: Duties of the Occupier) 137
Occupation Law (Part 2: Duties of the Occupied Population) 143

Chapter 9..149
Ceasefires, Armistices, and the White Flag.............................149
Ceasefires, Armistices, and the White Flag (Part 2).................152
Ceasefires, Armistices, and the White Flag (Part 3).................155
Courtesies Between Captains at Sea...157
Chapter 10..161
Neutrality and Collective Security (Part 1) 161
Neutrality and Collective Security (Part 2) 165
Neutrality and Non-International Armed Conflicts (Part 3) 170
Chapter 11..177
Enforcement and Accountability (Part 1) 177
Enforcement and Accountability (Part 2) 182
Conclusion 189
The Fragile Victory of Civilization 189
Notes on Sources..193
About the Author..197
Index 199
(Term List) 199
Appendix 205
The Lieber Instructions...205

PREFACE

This book is for everyone who can read. It is not a treatise. It is not a governmental or military manual. It is not even a scholarly commentary on the law of war. It is a little book that presents and reflects upon the highlights of this body of law in plain language—language accessible to ordinary interested people, soldiers and commanders, students, teachers, and more. It aims not only to inform, but also to stir the conscience of those who read it. The law of war is rooted not in abstractions but in the human, philosophical imperative to preserve dignity, even amid violence. My hope is that this volume will give its readers a clear sense of both the principles and the paradoxes of this difficult subject. The reflections here are shaped by a lifetime of study and experience. From my earliest legal training at the University of Toledo, where I first began to see the tension between military necessity and humanitarian restraint, to my graduate studies in Brussels, where I devoted my thesis to the protection of cultural property during armed conflict, the humanitarian dimensions of the law of war became ever clearer to me.

Earlier still, from 1978 to 1980, I had the privilege of working under Dr. Milan Bodi at the International Civil Defence Organization in Geneva. Reporting directly to him, I came to understand that international law—especially law designed to protect civilians in catastrophe—was not an academic exercise but a lifeline. In the early 1990s, as a lecturer in international law at the University of Toledo College of Law, I taught the law of international organizations. That teaching deepened my conviction that collective structures, whether states[1] or alliances, must be bound by law if they are to avoid slipping into barbarity. But what do we mean by the term "Law" when we speak of the law of war? I admit that it cannot possibly be the same as what we mean by the term "Law" when we are referring to the internal statutory and regulatory codes of states or nations. I

---

[1] The term "state" in international law and in diplomacy means "nation" rather than a component of a nation like "Tennessee." Other usages of the word "nation" such as "the Cherokee Nation" do not apply here, but would be a fascinating subject.

am confident that the meaning will become more apparent as our discussion progresses.

So, this book is the product of those years of work and study and inquiry. It does not aim to cover every detail of this peculiar body of law. Instead, it is an effort by an old lawyer trained in the subject to illuminate, for ordinary human beings of all walks of life, the essentials: the history, principles, protections, violations, and consequences that together form what we call the law of war.

INTRODUCTION

WHY THE LAW OF WAR MATTERS

When I first encountered the formal phrase "the law of war," I was struck by its paradox. How could there be a law about something that, at its very core, is the absence of law? War is organized violence: the suspension of the normal rules that govern human life. And yet, through centuries of conflict, there has always been a stubborn belief — sometimes honored, often violated — that even in war, some things must remain prohibited.

This paradox became more than an intellectual curiosity for me when I was a law student at the University of Toledo. There, I first began to see the tension between necessity and humanity: between what commanders believe they must do to succeed and what their conscience tells them not to do. Later, as a graduate student at the University of Brussels, that seed grew into full conviction. I devoted my thesis to one narrow corner of this vast field: the protection of cultural property during armed conflict.

It seemed to me that nothing revealed the tension of war and law more clearly than the question of whether libraries, museums, and religious structures could be shielded from the firestorm. Could marble cathedrals or priceless manuscripts — mute symbols of human identity — be spared in the furnace of destruction? That question haunted me and continues to haunt humanity.

Earlier still, from 1978 to 1980, I had the extraordinary privilege of working with Dr. Milan Bodi, then Secretary General of the International Civil Defence Organization in Geneva. The ICDO was and remains the foremost intergovernmental organization devoted to the protection of civilians in catastrophes of every kind, including armed conflict. Reporting directly to Dr. Bodi, I began to grasp the humanitarian underpinnings of international law in a way that no classroom alone could provide. Those years impressed upon me that the law of war is not a lawyer's abstraction, but a lifeline for civilians caught in fire. Sitting in Geneva, surrounded by delegates and experts from dozens of nations, I felt in my bones that these rules of protection that had developed over thousands of years were not academic exercises — they were survival itself.

The subjects of protection are many: combatants and commanders, from the most evil to the most innocent; culture and cultural monuments; borders and sovereignty; the civic structure and ordinary business of an occupied territory; civilians and their property; hospitals and other medical facilities; the religious components of warring parties, including battlefield chaplains; and even the burial rites and funerary equipment for the fallen. As one considers these subjects, it becomes apparent that all of humanity — the good and the bad, the just and the unjust — are in some measure protected by this law.

At its bedrock, the law of war is not merely about politics or treaties; it is grounded in the humanitarian urge that inheres in nearly all of us, the small inner voice that says compellingly: "You ought to do this, you ought not to do that." That urge is the pulse of civilization. It is the fragile thread that says human dignity must not be erased, even by war:

The Warrior

I am the king, the commander in chief.
He was a general of the army,
a man of the nation,
born of the nation,
protector of the nation,
protector of the people,
and of their land.
I summon the general,
and I tell him to go and kill the enemy.
And he goes,
and he kills,
he goes into their land
and he kills.
And then the enemy sends generals to our land,
and they kill.
They kill us.
I send for the general,

and his generals,

and they come and the general says to me,

"Your Majesty, we kill the enemy

and our enemy kills their enemy,

us,

and we are at war.

We kill them, they kill us,

we are at war."

And so I consider this war

and I ask the generals what it will take to win the war,

and the generals talk to me.

"We must kill many more of the enemy."

"We must destroy his food supply."

"We must make him want to end the war."

"We must degrade his weapons and stockpiles."

"We must have more and better spies than him."

"We must kill more of the enemy. We are not killing enough."

And one general says to me:

"My colleagues give good counsel.

But,

Your Majesty,

We cannot win this war.

No one can win this war.

Most wars are neither won nor lost;

Most wars are just stopped.

They kill, we kill, and then we all stop killing.

The war stops.

We do not win the war, we end the war.

When I say We,

Your Majesty,

that includes the enemy."

This general had my attention.

I wanted to hear more from him.

"What would you propose that we do to end this war?"

"Commander, Your Majesty,

you begin by heeding the counsel of my fellow generals.

You even heighten our effort,

as we move into this last phase of this war.

But we must know that the enemy will do the same.

As we continue to destroy and kill,

and be destroyed and killed,

by our enemy,

we will send word,

through our back channels,

that we can see,

in the distance,

an end to this war,

that there is no longer a need to kill and destroy.

Your Majesty,

we will tell our enemy,

through our back channels,

that perhaps soon our people can intermingle, and intermarry,

and trade goods,

and maybe,

maybe,

friendships destroyed by this war can be renewed,

and our descendants can live in peace,

without having to bear the memory of these horrors.

That is the message that you should send to our enemy.

But,

Your Majesty,

there is one principle,

one,

that I would humbly urge the king, Your Majesty, to consider,

and it is this:

It is easier to be enemies,

than it is to be friends.

The king must count the cost of friendship,
Your Majesty."
And so I listened to this subordinate general,
and I gathered him to my staff to counsel me.
Because of him
I can see an end to this war.

This poem first appeared in Joseph Edwards' collection homodeus: an introduction to the ineffable (2024). Though a meditation on the nature of war, it belongs equally to humanitarian law. It reminds us that most wars are not "won" but stopped. The law of war ensures that when killing ends, dignity and the possibility of friendship remain.

The law of war, then, is not a sterile body of rules but an attempt to hold onto humanity in the very moment when humanity is most endangered. Its history and principles, its protections and its demands, are the fragile gift that we inherit and must pass on. And to see where this gift began, we must turn back to the roots of restraint that long preceded modern treaties, to the ancient codes and customs that whispered, even then, that there must be limits in war.

CHAPTER 1

THE HISTORICAL ROOTS OF RESTRAINT

When people think of war, they imagine chaos and destruction, armies clashing, and the normal rules of life shattered. Yet from the earliest times, humanity has asked: must war be entirely lawless? Can even violence have rules? The very posing of those questions signals something profound — that humans have never been content to allow sheer brutality to reign unchecked. Across civilizations, cultures, and religions, the instinct has emerged to restrain excess, to place boundaries around violence, and to remind warriors and leaders alike that even enemies remain human.

The ancient codes are our first witnesses. In Babylon around the 18th century BCE, King Hammurabi inscribed his laws on a great stone stele, establishing proportionality as a governing principle. His famous line, "an eye for an eye," often misunderstood as brutality, was in fact a call for limits. The punishment must not exceed the harm. If a man put out the eye of another, his own eye would be put out — no more, no less. This prohibition of excessive vengeance was a step toward fairness, and in its own way an early rule of war. Hammurabi's code also punished those who mistreated captives or abandoned obligations of protection, hinting that war, too, must be governed by standards.

In India, the Mahābhārata, compiled over centuries and reaching its form around 400 BCE, contained passages that went beyond myth into moral injunctions. "Do not strike one who has laid down his arms," the text admonished. "Do not kill one who sleeps, or one who is afraid, or one who flees." Elsewhere it forbids poisoned and barbed weapons, recognizing that some tools of violence inflicted unnecessary suffering. This was the germ of a principle that would echo across millennia: weapons and tactics that cause suffering beyond military necessity are to be shunned.

Ancient Greece likewise developed customs to humanize conflict. Heralds and envoys were treated as inviolate, messengers not to be harmed even in the midst of battle. The Olympic truce allowed athletes and pilgrims safe passage during the games, suspending even bitter wars. Burial truces were observed, granting both sides a chance to collect and honor their dead. In Homer's *Iliad*, amid the carnage, Hector asks Achilles for a promise: "Give me your word that, when you have killed me, you will return my body to my people." Though Achilles refuses, the request itself shows that the Greeks understood restraint as an expectation, even when violated.

Rome built on these notions with its *jus fetiale*, a religious and legal system that governed the declaration of war and treaties of peace. The Roman orator Cicero in the 1st century BCE famously wrote: "Even war has its laws." His point was that legitimacy in conflict depended on observing certain restraints — that not everything was permitted, even in war. Rome punished those who killed ambassadors, a recognition that some roles had to be shielded from hostility. In such practices we see the faint outlines of what would become diplomatic immunity.

Religious traditions also pressed upon warriors the need for restraint. The Hebrew Scriptures, in Deuteronomy, contain the remarkable command not to destroy fruit trees during a siege: "When you besiege a city for a long time… you shall not destroy its trees by wielding an axe against them. You may eat from them, but you shall not cut them down." This principle, later expanded by rabbis into the doctrine of *bal tashchit* (do not waste), limited wanton destruction. Even in conquest, life-sustaining resources were not to be annihilated. This was more than prudence; it was a moral recognition that the earth's abundance should not be destroyed in anger.

In Islam's formative centuries, rules for the conduct of war were emphasized in both the Qur'an and the sayings of the Prophet Muhammad. In one report, he forbade the killing of women, children, and the elderly. Abu Bakr, the first caliph after Muhammad's death, instructed his armies: "Do not kill women or children or the aged, infirm. Do not cut down fruit trees, nor destroy inhabited places. Do not slaughter any of the enemy's sheep, cows, or camels, except for food." This direct order, carried down through the centuries, enshrined humanitarian principles at the heart of early Islamic warfare.

Christian thinkers also wrestled with the morality of war. Augustine of Hippo in the 5th century CE argued that war could only be just if waged with right intent — not cruelty or vengeance.

He saw war as tragic but sometimes necessary, always bound by moral limits. Centuries later, Thomas Aquinas added the principle of proportionality: force must be measured, and violence should never exceed what is required to secure peace. These principles infused medieval canon law and the ethos of chivalry, reminding knights that honor was bound up not only in bravery but also in restraint.

The Middle Ages saw both innovation and contradiction. In 10th-century France, the Church proclaimed the Peace and Truce of God. Certain persons — clergy, peasants, merchants — were to be immune from attack, and fighting was restricted on holy days. At the same time, the Crusades revealed humanity's brutal side. Chroniclers tell us that when Jerusalem was taken in 1099, the streets ran red with blood. Yet even this horror spurred renewed calls for restraint. After catastrophe, conscience reasserted itself.

Chivalric codes also shaped warfare. Knights were bound by honor to treat captured nobles humanely, often ransoming rather than killing them. This was not pure humanitarianism — it reflected the aristocratic solidarity of Europe's ruling classes — but it created a habit of sparing lives rather than destroying them. By the late Middle Ages, these customs spread beyond nobility, hinting at a broader humanitarian impulse.

As Europe entered the Renaissance and early modern period, a new generation of thinkers began to systematize what had long been instinct and custom. Francisco de Vitoria, a Dominican friar at Salamanca writing in the 1530s, confronted the brutal conquest of the New World. He acknowledged the sovereignty and rights of the indigenous peoples, insisting that conquest alone gave no license for cruelty. He argued that they had "true dominion, both public and private," and condemned enslavement and abuse. Vitoria's teaching was radical in its time — it pierced through the justifications of empire and announced that law must bind conqueror as well as conquered.

Alberico Gentili, an Italian jurist exiled to England, published *De Jure Belli* in 1598. He emphasized that war should not be lawless, that treatment of prisoners and civilians must be governed by rules. Gentili's famous dictum, "Let war be lawful, so that peace may be just," reflected his conviction that cruelty in conflict poisoned the very peace it was meant to secure.

Then came Hugo Grotius, often called the father of international law. His *De Jure Belli ac Pacis* (1625) drew from Roman law, theology, and philosophy to argue that sovereigns were bound by law even in war. Grotius declared: "The binding force of law does not cease in war." He insisted that captured enemies were not mere spoils, but human beings entitled to dignity. Though his influence took centuries to mature, Grotius laid the intellectual foundation of modern humanitarian law.

The Enlightenment inherited these arguments and began to universalize them. Philosophers like Immanuel Kant would later envision a "perpetual peace" founded on republican government and federation of states. Though that dream proved elusive, the moral trajectory of restraint gained new momentum.

The 19th century brought a crisis and a turning point. On June 24, 1859, the armies of France, Sardinia, and Austria clashed near the Italian town of Solferino. The battle left some 40,000 dead and wounded strewn across the fields. A Swiss businessman, Henri Dunant, happened upon the carnage. He was horrified to find the wounded left untended, moaning in agony, as military units pressed on. Dunant rallied local villagers, crying out "Tutti fratelli" — "we are all brothers" — and organized care for the wounded regardless of side. His book, *A Memory of Solferino* (1862), shocked Europe and ignited a movement. Within two years, the International Committee of the Red Cross was born. And in 1864, the First Geneva Convention was signed, binding nations to care for the wounded and respect medical personnel and facilities. It was the first modern multilateral treaty on humanitarian law, and it grew directly from one man's conscience awakened on a battlefield.

Across the Atlantic, another milestone unfolded. In the midst of the American Civil War, President Abraham Lincoln commissioned Francis Lieber, a Prussian émigré and Columbia professor, to draft rules for Union armies. The result was General Orders No. 100, issued in 1863, known as the Lieber Instructions. It was a remarkable document, blending military necessity with humanitarian restraint. It prohibited torture, cruelty, and the use of poison. It declared that "military necessity does not admit of cruelty — that is, the infliction of suffering for the sake of suffering." It condemned perfidy, such as feigning surrender, and prohibited "no quarter" orders that left no room for mercy or surrender. It even included protection for cultural property, declaring that classical works of art and science "must be secured against all avoidable injury." The Lieber Instructions influenced not only the conduct of the Civil War but also subsequent European treaties, and it became a cornerstone of the modern law of war. I consider it to have been so central to the development of the law of war that I have attached the full text of the document at the end of this book. In reading it, one should keep in mind that the Lieber Instructions were not created from nothing. They gathered, organized, and presented a succinct current statement of the humanitarian norms governing the conduct of war, as they had developed since antiquity.

The Hague Peace Conferences of 1899 and 1907 marked the next great step. Dozens of nations gathered to codify rules for war and peace. The Hague Conventions addressed the declaration of war, treatment of prisoners, protection of civilians, and restrictions on weapons. Expanding bullets — "dum-dums" — were banned as causing unnecessary suffering. Poison gas was prohibited, though tragically used later in World War I. Article 46 of the 1907 Convention required respect for family honor and private property in occupied territories. Though cynics later derided The Hague as naïve, its norms set enduring expectations. When those rules were broken — in Verdun, in Auschwitz — the world recognized the breach precisely because The Hague had given us standards to measure against.

These developments — Dunant's cry of fraternity, Lieber's balance of necessity and humanity, The Hague's codifications — did not eliminate war's cruelty. But they established the principle that war was not outside law. They told commanders and soldiers alike that conscience and law walked with them into battle. They declared to civilians that even amid the roar of cannon, their lives and dignity still mattered.

By the close of the 19th century, the idea that war must be restrained had become more than custom or isolated moral teaching. It had become law, codified in treaties and embodied in international organizations. Yet it remained fragile, dependent on the will of states to honor their promises. The Hague Conventions signaled hope, but the looming conflicts of the 20th century would put that hope to the severest test.

The First World War broke out in 1914, and the optimism of The Hague quickly collided with industrial slaughter. Poison gas was unleashed on the Western Front despite prohibitions; at Ypres in 1915, chlorine clouds rolled over the trenches, searing lungs and blinding thousands. Machine guns and heavy artillery inflicted casualties on a scale unimaginable in previous wars. At Verdun in 1916, France and Germany hurled millions of shells across no man's land, and hundreds of thousands of soldiers died in a battle of attrition. Yet even amid horror, the presence of existing law mattered. Atrocities were condemned not just morally but legally, for The Hague had given language and framework to outrage.

The war also showed the importance of humanitarian institutions. The Red Cross organized relief, visited prisoners of war, and carried mail between captives and their families. Its presence testified that even in the most mechanized war to date, the cry of "tutti fratelli" (We are all brothers) still resonated. In 1929, learning from the lessons of World War I, states adopted the Geneva Convention relative to the treatment of prisoners of war, extending legal protection to captives who had too often been neglected or abused.

The interwar years saw further developments. The League of Nations sought to make war itself illegal, enshrining collective security in its covenant. The Kellogg–Briand Pact of 1928, signed by major powers, renounced war as an instrument of national policy. Cynics dismissed it, for it lacked enforcement, but its principle — that aggressive war is unlawful — would become crucial later in Nuremberg.

World War II tested the law of war as never before. Nazi Germany and Imperial Japan unleashed total war, targeting civilians, waging campaigns of extermination, and disregarding virtually every humanitarian restraint. Yet precisely because these acts violated established law, they could later be prosecuted as crimes. At Nuremberg in 1945–46, leading Nazi officials were tried not only for crimes against peace but also for war crimes and crimes against humanity. The tribunal declared: "War is essentially an evil thing... To initiate a war of aggression is not only an international crime; it is the supreme international crime." The Tokyo Tribunal followed, holding Japanese leaders to account. For the first time in history, individuals were judged and punished by an international court for violations of the law of war.

The world responded by strengthening the Geneva framework. In 1949, four new Geneva Conventions were adopted, addressing the wounded and sick, prisoners of war, and most significantly, the protection of civilians. Later, Additional Protocols in 1977 expanded protections further, adapting to modern conflicts and reaffirming that humanitarian imperatives are the bedrock of international law. The prohibition of genocide, adopted in the 1948 Convention, spoke directly to the Holocaust and aimed to prevent its recurrence. The law of war was no longer a fragile set of customs; it had become a body of binding treaties, with near-universal acceptance.

The trajectory from Hammurabi's stone stele to Geneva's conference halls is jagged but unmistakable.

Every era added to the fabric of restraint. Ancient epics, religious injunctions, medieval customs, Renaissance scholarship, Enlightenment philosophy, and 19th-century humanitarian movements — all contributed threads. Catastrophe often spurred progress: Solferino birthed the Red Cross, the Civil War produced the Lieber Instructions, World War I shaped prisoner protections, and World War II produced tribunals and conventions. Each horror, paradoxically, deepened the world's commitment to prevent its repetition.

Yet fragility remains. The 20th and 21st centuries have seen violations as terrible as those in earlier times — from Cambodia to Rwanda, from Srebrenica to Syria. Each time, however, the law of war has served as a measure, a language of condemnation, and a standard for accountability. Its existence allows us to name atrocities not merely as moral outrages but as legal crimes. Its presence affirms that humanity has not surrendered to barbarism, that even in the darkest times we insist on rules, however often broken.

Thus, the historical roots of restraint remind us of two enduring truths: first, that the impulse to limit war is as ancient as war itself; and second, that law grows in response to suffering. The story of the law of war is not a straight line of progress but a cycle of horror, reflection, and renewed resolve. And it is in that cycle — painful, imperfect, but real — that we find the fragile continuity of civilization.

CHAPTER 2

DEFINING THE LAW OF WAR, PART 1: VOCABULARY AND PURPOSE

When we speak of the "law of war," we are already speaking in paradox. The very phrase seems to contradict itself. War, after all, is the breakdown of order, the eruption of violence that disregards the norms of peace. Yet even as far back as Cicero, there was recognition that war cannot be entirely lawless. Cicero, writing in the 1st century BCE, observed that "silent enim leges inter arma"—"laws fall silent in the midst of arms." The phrase has often been repeated as though it were a license for barbarism, but Cicero himself did not mean that law ceased to exist in wartime. Rather, he was pointing to the constant tension between necessity and restraint, a tension that still defines the field that many now call international humanitarian law.

Modern vocabulary reflects this tension. Lawyers and soldiers speak of three overlapping terms: the law of war, the law of armed conflict, and international humanitarian law (IHL). Each term reflects not only a different audience, but also a slightly different emphasis. The "law of war" is the oldest phrase, plain and blunt, with the paradox embedded in its very name. It is the language of common sense: rules for the battlefield. The "law of armed conflict," favored by militaries, has a more clinical tone. It implies that war is a type of conflict among others, and that law can bring order even here. "International humanitarian law" is the most modern and technical term, used by scholars, the International Committee of the Red Cross (ICRC), and the United Nations. It emphasizes not war, but humanity. It shifts the focus from strategy to suffering, from victory to dignity.

But however we name it, this body of law must be carefully distinguished from another branch of international law: jus ad bellum, the law of when war may be initiated. The United Nations Charter makes this distinction clear. Article 2(4) prohibits the use of force by states except in cases of self-defense or Security Council authorization. Article 51 preserves the "inherent right of individual or collective self-defense." That is the realm of jus ad bellum: the legitimacy of going to war in the first place. By contrast, the law of war—jus in bello—applies once war has begun, regardless of who started it. Soldiers and civilians must be protected even if their side is the aggressor. This distinction is not merely academic. When NATO intervened in Kosovo in 1999, lawyers debated endlessly whether the bombing campaign was justified under jus ad bellum. But at the same time, NATO commanders were bound by jus in bello: they had to distinguish civilian from military targets, to calibrate proportionality, and to accept accountability for errors. In Iraq in 2003, similar debates played out. Whatever one thought of the invasion's legality, the treatment of prisoners, the conduct of sieges, and the protection of hospitals fell under the law of war.

This is the heart of the paradox. The law of war does not pretend to prevent war itself. It does not abolish killing, nor does it claim to make violence humane in any absolute sense. Rather, it accepts that war exists and seeks to draw lines within it. In this sense it is a "law of limits." Its very existence is a recognition that unrestrained war devours humanity, while restrained war, though still terrible, leaves space for civilization to survive.

The purpose of the law of war is therefore not utopian but practical. It is meant to protect those who do not, or no longer, participate in hostilities, and to regulate the means and methods of warfare. Its twin foundations are military necessity and humanity. Military necessity allows actions necessary to weaken the enemy's armed forces, but humanity forbids those actions that cause superfluous injury or unnecessary suffering. This tension—between what is necessary and what is humane—runs through every rule, every treaty, every tribunal decision. It is the fulcrum on which war and law balance.

Examples illustrate this better than theory. In World War II, the German High Command often invoked "necessity" to justify scorched-earth retreats and reprisals against civilians. Yet at Nuremberg, the tribunal rejected necessity as an excuse for cruelty. The law, it said, permits destruction only when it contributes directly to defeating the enemy's military capacity—not when it punishes populations or annihilates culture. The claim that the atomic bombing of Hiroshima and Nagasaki was justified as military necessity remains one of the most contested arguments in legal history. Was there truly no other way to secure surrender? Could proportionality be squared with the obliteration of entire cities? These debates reveal the constant struggle between the two pillars.

The vocabulary of the law of war also includes key distinctions that shape every battlefield decision. Who is a combatant? Who is a civilian? What is a lawful target? The answers define life and death. Consider a farmer in Afghanistan who tends his fields by day but plants improvised explosive devices at night. Is he a civilian or a combatant? The law says he is protected until he directly participates in hostilities, but once he does, he loses that protection. What about a school used to store weapons? The law says it becomes a military objective, but only while it is so used, and only if attacking it is proportionate. These distinctions may appear abstract in textbooks, but in real conflicts they are matters of seconds and lives.

The paradox, again, is that even the most cynical violators rarely admit to ignoring the law altogether. Instead, they reinterpret it, bend it, or claim compliance. When Russian forces bombed civilian infrastructure in Ukraine, official statements insisted the targets were "dual-use" or "command and control" centers. When the United States bombed a hospital in Kunduz, Afghanistan, in 2015, it called the strike a mistake, not an attack on civilians. Hypocrisy, as the French moralist La Rochefoucauld once observed, is the homage vice pays to virtue. That belligerents feel compelled to justify themselves in the vocabulary of the law of war proves the law's enduring power, even when it is violated.

One final point about purpose must be emphasized. The law of war protects not only civilians but also combatants themselves. This is sometimes forgotten. Soldiers may kill, but once captured, they may not be tortured. They may be detained, but they may not be humiliated. Henri Dunant, the founder of the Red Cross, understood this when he wrote after Solferino that "you have no enemies captured, only men disarmed." To recognize humanity in the enemy is to preserve one's own humanity as well. The law of war thus does not only protect the innocent; it also shields the guilty from annihilation, and commanders from moral abdication. It keeps open the possibility that after the guns fall silent, reconciliation remains possible.

The vocabulary of war and law, then, is not just a matter of words. It reflects centuries of effort to discipline violence without pretending to abolish it. It is the grammar of restraint in a world that so often forgets restraint. It distinguishes between the legality of going to war and the legality of fighting it. It balances necessity against humanity. And it insists, paradoxically yet persistently, that even war must have laws.

Defining the Law of War, Part 2: Sources of Authority

If the law of war is to be more than a moral aspiration, it must rest on sources of authority that make it recognizable and binding. Over centuries, those sources have evolved from ancient custom to modern treaties, from battlefield honor to judicial precedent. Today, they fall broadly into four categories: customary law, treaty law, judicial decisions, and the writings of respected commentators. Together, they form the backbone of what soldiers, commanders, and lawyers mean when they invoke "the law of war."

Customary law is the oldest and most resilient. Long before treaties were drafted, warriors observed certain practices not because they were written down, but because they were accepted as binding by tradition. The prohibition against killing envoys or heralds is a classic example. In ancient Greece, to harm a messenger was to invite disgrace and retaliation. The rule persisted through Rome and into medieval Europe, becoming so ingrained that even modern armies treat the protection of diplomats as obvious. Likewise, the burial truce—temporary halts in fighting to collect and honor the dead—was practiced long before it was codified. These customs became binding precisely because they were widely accepted and consistently observed. Today, the International Court of Justice and the International Committee of the Red Cross both affirm that customary law remains binding on states whether or not they have ratified particular treaties.

Treaty law, by contrast, is the product of deliberate negotiation and agreement. The 1864 Geneva Convention, for example, arose from Henri Dunant's outrage at Solferino. It bound its signatories to respect and protect the wounded and to recognize the neutrality of medical personnel. That slim text—just ten articles—set in motion a cascade of treaties that followed: the 1906 revision, the 1929 conventions on prisoners of war, and the sweeping 1949 Geneva Conventions that remain the cornerstone of humanitarian law today. Four separate Geneva Conventions now address the wounded and sick on land, the wounded and shipwrecked at sea, prisoners of war, and civilians under occupation. Later, the 1977 Additional Protocols expanded protections to victims of internal armed conflicts and prohibited indiscriminate attacks. Each treaty builds upon the last, a continual growth of human effort to limit the horrors of war.

The Hague Conventions of 1899 and 1907 illustrate another aspect of treaty law: the regulation not of victims but of methods and means. They addressed declarations of war, rights of neutrals, the conduct of sieges, and the prohibition of poison. Article 23 of the 1907 Hague Regulations explicitly forbids "the employment of arms, projectiles, or material calculated to cause unnecessary suffering." This language remains at the heart of modern weapons reviews. When new technologies emerge—nuclear arms, cluster munitions, autonomous drones—lawyers ask whether their use would cause superfluous injury or unnecessary suffering, a test first articulated at The Hague.

Judicial decisions, while rarer, give life and authority to both custom and treaty. The Nuremberg Trials after World War II remain the most famous example. The Tribunal declared that individuals, including heads of state, could be held personally accountable for war crimes. It rejected the defense of "just following orders," insisting that soldiers have a duty to refuse commands that are manifestly illegal. In one striking passage, the Tribunal stated: "Crimes against international law are committed by men, not by abstract entities, and only by punishing individuals who commit such crimes can the provisions of international law be enforced." The principles of Nuremberg, later adopted by the United Nations, established that the law of war binds not only states but also individuals.

The Tokyo Tribunal, though often criticized for procedural shortcomings, reinforced similar norms in the Pacific theater. Later, the International Criminal Tribunal for the former Yugoslavia (ICTY) and the International Criminal Tribunal for Rwanda (ICTR) built upon these precedents. At The Hague in the

1990s, commanders like General Tihomir Blaškić were prosecuted for failing to prevent atrocities. In Rwanda, Jean-Paul Akayesu was convicted not only for war crimes but also for genocide, showing how the law of war intersects with broader human rights protections. These judicial interventions proved that humanitarian law is not a dead letter. Courts could interpret, apply, and enforce it, even decades after Nuremberg.

Finally, the writings of commentators—sometimes called the doctrine of the "publicists"—form a recognized source of law. Hugo Grotius's *De Jure Belli ac Pacis* (1625) is perhaps the most influential. Grotius insisted that war must be governed by law because even enemies are part of the common society of humankind. Alberico Gentili, earlier, had argued that Christian and non-Christian alike shared rights in war, challenging the idea that religion justified conquest. In the 20th century, Jean Pictet of the ICRC became the great expositor of the Geneva Conventions, whose commentaries are still cited by courts and scholars alike. While commentators do not create binding rules, their writings clarify, systematize, and sometimes inspire the codification of custom into treaty.

Taken together, these sources establish a body of law that is both flexible and enduring. Customary law ensures continuity across centuries; treaties provide clarity and precision; courts enforce accountability; commentators interpret and guide. When a modern commander consults a military manual, these sources converge. The U.S. Army Field Manual 27-10, for example, explicitly incorporates Hague and Geneva rules, cites Nuremberg principles, and reflects customary prohibitions on perfidy and reprisals. When NATO forces conducted operations in Libya in 2011, their lawyers reviewed every strike against these same touchstones.

The authority of the law of war, then, does not rest on a single pillar but on a constellation of sources. This constellation reflects the hybrid nature of the law itself: both ancient and modern, both customary and codified, both judicial and doctrinal. Its very resilience lies in this hybridity. Should a state repudiate a treaty, customary law still binds it. Should a commander claim no precedent exists, commentators and court rulings can be invoked. The law of war is not as rigid as domestic criminal codes, but neither is it mere aspiration. It is a living body of norms, constantly shaped by practice, treaty, judgment, and thought.

Defining the Law of War, Part 3: Core Principles

The law of war, drawn from custom, treaties, judicial rulings, and commentary, is not a shapeless body of rules. It coheres around several core principles that recur across centuries and cultures: distinction, proportionality, necessity, and humanity. These principles are the compass points by which commanders navigate the fog of war, and they remain as relevant today as they were in the age of Grotius or Lieber.

The principle of distinction is the cornerstone. It requires parties to distinguish between combatants and civilians, and to direct operations only against the former. This idea, though deceptively simple, is deeply rooted. As early as the *Mahābhārata*, warriors were forbidden to attack the unarmed, the sleeping, or those who surrendered. In medieval Europe, the Peace and Truce of God movements sought to protect peasants, clergy, and merchants. Today,

Article 48 of Additional Protocol I to the Geneva Conventions states the rule with clarity: "The Parties to the conflict shall at all times distinguish between the civilian population and combatants… and accordingly shall direct their operations only against military objectives." The clarity of the principle belies the difficulty of applying it in practice. Guerrilla warfare, urban insurgency, and modern terrorism blur the line between soldier and civilian. Yet the obligation remains, and failure to observe it has been the basis for prosecutions from Nuremberg to the ICTY.

Closely tied to distinction is proportionality. The law recognizes that even legitimate attacks may cause incidental harm to civilians or civilian property. But such harm must not be excessive in relation to the concrete and direct military advantage anticipated. This principle crystallized in the Hague Regulations of 1907, which required that belligerents respect family honor, civilian property, and religious institutions. In modern times, proportionality has been tested repeatedly. The NATO bombing of Belgrade in 1999, for example, drew criticism when a television station was struck, killing civilians. NATO argued that the station was a legitimate command-and-control node; others questioned whether the civilian cost outweighed the advantage gained. Proportionality is rarely a matter of arithmetic. It demands judgment, and in practice, it is one of the most litigated and debated principles in humanitarian law.

The principle of necessity tempers restraint with realism. It acknowledges that war is, at its core, about defeating an enemy. Actions that are necessary to achieve a legitimate military objective are permitted—so long as they do not violate other prohibitions. The Lieber Instructions of 1863 articulated this balance with unusual clarity: "Military necessity admits of all direct destruction of life or limb of armed enemies, and of other persons whose destruction is incidentally unavoidable in the armed contests of war; it does not admit of cruelty." This distinction between necessity and cruelty remains vital. Destroying an enemy bridge to prevent reinforcements may be necessary; massacring prisoners is not. In modern practice, the necessity principle underlies weapons reviews: new arms must be evaluated for whether their destructive effect is necessary to disable the enemy or whether they cause gratuitous suffering.

Finally, the principle of humanity is the constant thread. It insists that even in the pursuit of victory, there are lines that must not be crossed. The Hague Conventions explicitly forbade poison, treachery, and attacks on undefended towns. Geneva forbids torture, degrading treatment, and the denial of medical care. Humanity underlies every other principle. Distinction without humanity would be a sterile rule; proportionality without humanity would be mere calculus. Humanity ensures that the law of war is not only about effectiveness but about the preservation of human dignity.

A fifth principle, sometimes invoked, is that of honor or chivalry. Though less codified, it has long influenced the culture of armies. The idea that combat should be fought openly and that perfidy—feigning surrender to ambush the enemy, for example—is forbidden, derives from this sense of honor. Article 37 of Additional Protocol I explicitly prohibits perfidy, codifying what was once a knightly ethic.

These principles are not abstract philosophy. They are lived realities on the battlefield. When a drone operator in Nevada is ordered to strike a compound in Afghanistan, the law of war requires that distinction and proportionality be assessed before the missile is released. When a commander in Ukraine orders artillery fire near a city, necessity must be weighed against humanity. The law of war does not eliminate suffering, but it sets boundaries within which war may be waged without descending into total barbarism.

PART 4: COMBATANTS AND NON-COMBATANTS

War draws a line through humanity, dividing the world into those who fight and those who do not. Yet the law of war does not leave that line entirely to the whims of generals or governments. Instead, it sets boundaries, defining who is a combatant, who is a civilian, and what rights attach to each category. This distinction is at the heart of humanitarian law. Without it, the battlefield would be a free-for-all, and no one—soldier or civilian—could claim any protection at all.

A lawful combatant is not just anyone who picks up a weapon. The law insists on a certain discipline and openness. Combatants must belong to an organized force under a responsible chain of command. They must wear a distinctive sign or uniform recognizable at a distance. They must carry arms openly, not concealed like assassins. And crucially, they must respect the laws and customs of war themselves. These conditions, first set out in The Hague Regulations of 1907 and reaffirmed in the Geneva Conventions, are meant to ensure that combat remains, at least in theory, a contest between opposing armies rather than a war of shadows against civilians.

In exchange for meeting these conditions, combatants earn a powerful legal protection: prisoner-of-war status. If captured, they may not be executed simply for fighting. They must be treated humanely, provided food, shelter, and medical care, and released at the close of hostilities. This principle, codified in the Third Geneva Convention of 1949, is one of the most significant advances of humanitarian law. A soldier who lays down his arms and falls into enemy hands does not forfeit his humanity.

Civilians, on the other hand, are shielded from direct attack. They are not to be targeted unless and until they take a direct part in hostilities—by picking up a rifle, planting a bomb, or directly serving the enemy in some way. Even then, their loss of protection lasts only for as long as they are engaged in such acts. Once they cease, the shield returns. The principle was tested repeatedly in modern conflicts. In Vietnam, insurgents who blended with the local population posed agonizing questions for U.S. forces: who was a farmer and who was a guerrilla? Similar dilemmas have recurred in Afghanistan and Iraq, where insurgents did not wear uniforms or distinguish themselves from the population. The law itself never changed—the civilian remains protected unless directly participating—but the fog of war made its application far more difficult.

History provides sobering reminders of what happens when these distinctions collapse. During the Boer War at the turn of the 20th century, British forces responded to guerrilla tactics by interning large numbers of civilians in camps, a practice that sparked outrage and debate over collective punishment. In World War II, Nazi reprisals against occupied populations—executions of hostages in France, massacres in the Balkans—flagrantly ignored the civilian-combatant divide. These were not just atrocities; they were legal crimes, and after the war, the Nuremberg Tribunal specifically recognized that targeting civilians was a violation of the laws and customs of war.

The International Criminal Tribunal for the Former Yugoslavia (ICTY) built on this foundation when it ruled against individuals who blurred the line between combatants and civilians. In the *Tadić* case (1997), the tribunal held that even in non-international armed conflicts, the fundamental principle remains: civilians are protected from attack unless directly engaged in fighting. That judgment closed a gap in the law, making clear that the distinction applies not only to great wars between states but also to civil wars and insurgencies, which are now the dominant form of conflict worldwide.

The treatment of prisoners of war has also been a consistent barometer of civilization in war. At Nuremberg, one of the charges against German commanders was the execution and mistreatment of Soviet POWs, hundreds of thousands of whom were starved or shot. In more recent history, the United States' detention of suspected Taliban and al-Qaeda members at Guantánamo Bay raised global debates over who qualifies as a combatant. The Bush administration's invention of the category of "unlawful enemy combatant" was widely criticized as an attempt to sidestep Geneva protections. International law does not deny that irregular fighters exist, but it insists that even those outside the narrow definition of lawful combatants retain certain basic protections, such as freedom from torture or summary execution.

This balance between military necessity and humanitarian protection is precarious, but it is vital. The line between combatant and non-combatant may be blurred by tactics, technology, or politics, yet the law demands that it be drawn. Without it, every man, woman, and child in a conflict zone would be a fair target. With it, imperfect though its enforcement may be, a measure of humanity survives even in the midst of destruction.

PART 5: PERFIDY AND QUARTER

Among the most deeply rooted prohibitions in the law of war are those against perfidy and denial of quarter. These are not abstract technicalities but matters that go to the heart of trust, honor, and the possibility of restraint even in the midst of killing.

Perfidy, in its simplest form, is betrayal. The Hague Regulations of 1907 and later the Additional Protocol I of 1977 both define it as acts that invite the confidence of an adversary under the guise of legal protection, only to betray that confidence. Pretending to surrender in order to ambush, feigning incapacitation by wounds, or misusing protected symbols like the Red Cross are classic examples. When a soldier waves a white flag, the law insists that it must mean surrender, not deception. If such gestures lose their meaning, the fragile trust that allows combatants to spare lives collapses, and war descends into unrestrained savagery.

The consequences of perfidy are severe. A perfidious act strips the perpetrator of combatant protections. Those captured after committing perfidy may be prosecuted and punished, sometimes even by summary battlefield justice if the act is clear and ongoing. At Nuremberg, several German commanders were tried for misusing protected symbols—dressing soldiers in civilian clothes or Red Cross garb to infiltrate enemy lines. The tribunal treated these as serious war crimes, recognizing that they endangered not only immediate opponents but the entire system of protection.

Closely related is the prohibition on denial of quarter. To "give no quarter" is to refuse mercy to those who surrender, to declare that no prisoners will be taken. This principle has been rejected for centuries, appearing explicitly in the Lieber Instructions of 1863, which stated in Article 60: "It is against the usage of modern war to resolve, to give no quarter." The Hague Conventions reinforced it, and today it is enshrined in Article 40 of Additional Protocol I: "It is prohibited to order that there shall be no survivors."

The rationale is simple but profound: if surrender does not guarantee survival, then no soldier will ever lay down his arms, and battles will spiral into mutual slaughter. The denial of quarter removes the very mechanism that limits bloodshed. History shows the consequences. During World War II, Japanese forces were notorious for refusing quarter, particularly in the Pacific theater, leading to fanatical resistance and staggering casualties on both sides. At the same time, Allied forces faced moral and legal debates over whether to reciprocate. The law was clear: mercy to the surrendered is not optional; it is binding.

Modern courts have continued to enforce these rules. The International Criminal Tribunal for Rwanda convicted commanders who had ordered massacres under the guise of eliminating enemies, making clear that a general declaration of "kill them all" is unlawful even in the chaos of civil war. In the ICTY's *Martić* case, the shelling of civilian areas under false pretenses of military necessity was treated as perfidy in practice, an abuse of trust that crossed into crime.

Perfidy and denial of quarter illustrate how the law of war protects not only civilians but also combatants. A soldier must be able to trust that surrender is meaningful, that a white flag is not a trick, that a red cross marks healing and not ambush. Without such trust, the incentives for restraint collapse. With them, however fragile, a minimum of honor survives on the battlefield. They are reminders that even in the most brutal circumstances, law and humanity insist that deceit and slaughter without mercy are beyond the pale.

Part 6: Necessity, Proportionality, and Humanity

The law of war is built on a tension that never goes away: the need to fight and the need to restrain. Out of that tension emerge three pillars—necessity, proportionality, and humanity—that guide commanders and constrain their choices. Each is rooted in centuries of thought and practice, and each is both indispensable and vulnerable to abuse.

Necessity is often the first claim a commander makes. It is the principle that military action must be directed toward a legitimate military objective, and that destruction for its own sake is forbidden. Francis Lieber wrote in 1863 that "military necessity admits of all direct destruction of life or limb of armed enemies... but it does not admit of cruelty." In other words, necessity allows you to fight, but only insofar as fighting serves a real military aim. History shows what happens when necessity becomes a cloak for vengeance. During the Second World War, some German commanders justified scorched-earth tactics in retreat by claiming necessity, when in truth the goal was terror. At Nuremberg, this defense failed; the tribunal made clear that necessity is not a license for destruction but a test of legitimacy.

Closely linked is proportionality. If necessity answers the question "why act," proportionality asks "how much." The principle demands that even when a military target is legitimate, the harm to civilians and civilian objects must not be excessive in relation to the anticipated military advantage. This balancing test is among the most difficult in law. Consider the Allied bombing of Monte Cassino in 1944. Commanders believed the monastery had been fortified by German troops, and so they leveled it from the air. In fact, the Germans had not occupied it until after the bombing. Thousands of cultural treasures were destroyed, and the military advantage was nil. The lesson still echoes: proportionality requires commanders to weigh evidence carefully and err on the side of restraint.

Humanity runs through both principles. It insists that suffering not required by military necessity is forbidden. The prohibition on torture, the ban on weapons designed to cause superfluous injury, and the protection of civilians all derive from this impulse. It is why expanding bullets, designed to shred tissue, were banned at The Hague. It is why chemical gas, after the horrors of Ypres in 1915, was outlawed in the 1925 Geneva Protocol. Humanity is the voice that says, "Even in war, cruelty is not an option."

These principles are not theoretical. They have been enforced in courts. The International Criminal Tribunal for the Former Yugoslavia, in the *Kupreškić* case, found that attacks on villages in Bosnia violated proportionality when entire communities were shelled with no genuine military objective. The judgment reaffirmed that proportionality is not abstract but binding. Similarly, the ICTR in the *Akayesu* case recognized that attacks on civilians in Rwanda were both unnecessary and inhumane, meeting the threshold of crimes against humanity.

Yet necessity, proportionality, and humanity are not self-executing. They depend on commanders making choices under stress. They depend on training, doctrine, and culture. They depend, in the end, on the moral courage to say "enough." Frans de Pauw, my professor in Brussels, used to remind us that when enforcement fails, when courts are silent and politics protect the guilty, sometimes the only weapon left is "the mobilization of shame." The world's gaze can still matter. It can call out cruelty and insist that humanity not vanish entirely from the battlefield.

Together, these three principles are not abstractions but the compass of the law of war. They do not eliminate violence, but they keep it from devouring everything. They remind us that victory purchased at the cost of our own humanity is no victory at all.

The principles of necessity, proportionality, and humanity shape not only decisions about targets but also the very tools used in combat. Weapons, after all, are not neutral; some are designed to kill efficiently, others to terrorize, maim, or destroy indiscriminately. The law of war draws a line between what can be used and what must be banned.

The first restrictions came with the Hague Conventions. Expanding, or "dum-dum," bullets were prohibited in 1899 because they shattered inside the body, causing grievous wounds disproportionate to their military utility. Chemical weapons, after their horrifying debut at Ypres in 1915, were outlawed in the 1925 Geneva Protocol. Yet despite this ban, gas was used again during the Second World War in extermination camps and later in conflicts like the Iran-Iraq War. Each time, the world's conscience was stirred anew, and legal prohibitions grew stronger. By the 1993 Chemical Weapons Convention, nearly every nation in the world had agreed that gas and toxins must never again be part of human conflict.

Other treaties followed. Biological weapons were banned under the 1972 Biological Weapons Convention. In the late 20th century, campaigns by civil society helped achieve the 1997 Mine Ban Treaty and the 2008 Convention on Cluster Munitions, both outlawing weapons whose effects linger long after the fighting stops, killing civilians and children decades later. More recently, a 1995 protocol prohibited blinding laser weapons, recognizing that technologies designed to maim without killing serve no legitimate military purpose.

Beyond weapons, the law also protects what is sacred to human identity: culture. The 1954 Hague

Convention for the Protection of Cultural Property, drafted in response to the devastation of Europe's treasures in World War II, forbids the targeting of monuments, libraries, and works of art. The blue-and-white shield symbol created by the convention marks protected sites, reminding armies that a church, a manuscript, or a statue is not a combatant. When the Old Bridge of Mostar was destroyed during the Balkan wars, or when ISIS demolished Palmyra, the outrage showed how deeply humanity feels these losses. They are not just stones or ruins but embodiments of memory, dignity, and meaning.

Still, the temptation to misuse protected objects persists. Hospitals and cultural sites have been cynically used as shields, drawing return fire and blurring the line between lawful and unlawful attack. Here the law is clear: protection is lost if a site is used for hostile purposes, but commanders must weigh carefully, for striking a hospital or a museum, even when misused, risks both moral and legal disaster.

In the end, the law of war is a fragile architecture built on trust, custom, and conscience. It is not perfect. Violations are frequent. Cynics dismiss it as a fig leaf for brutality. Yet its existence transforms the battlefield. It means that a white flag has meaning, that a red cross signifies care, that a surrender can be trusted, that certain weapons are off limits. It means that a commander is accountable, that cruelty can be punished, that humanity, however scarred, has not vanished.

The law of war does not end wars, but it tempers them. It does not abolish suffering, but it insists that suffering must not be unlimited. It draws a line—sometimes faint, sometimes contested—between necessity and savagery. And in that line lies the fragile possibility of dignity, even amid destruction.

Chapter 3

The Sources of Authority (Part 1: Treaties and Conventions)

The most visible and concrete sources of the law of war are its treaties and conventions. These documents, solemnly negotiated and signed by states, take the instincts of restraint that grew out of custom and crystallize them into binding promises. They are the points where the voice of conscience is transcribed into articles, sections, and protocols. Some of these agreements are obscure and technical, while others, like the Geneva Conventions, have become part of our moral vocabulary. Together they show how humanity has tried, again and again, to make law speak even in the midst of arms.

The Hague Conventions of 1899 and 1907 marked the first great effort to create a comprehensive, international framework for the conduct of hostilities. Delegates from dozens of nations gathered in the Dutch capital to negotiate rules about how wars should be fought. The first conference in 1899 produced agreements on the peaceful settlement of disputes, the laws and customs of land warfare, and prohibitions on certain weapons, such as expanding bullets. The second conference in 1907 deepened these commitments, producing the Hague Regulations that remain a cornerstone of the law of war. Article 23 forbade treachery, and Article 46 required respect for family honor, lives, and property of civilians. Though the Hague Conventions did not prevent the carnage of the First World War, they provided a framework for judging its excesses and for shaping postwar reforms. They remain, more than a century later, a touchstone of international humanitarian law.

If The Hague was about codifying the customs of land warfare, Geneva was about human suffering. The first Geneva Convention, adopted in 1864, focused narrowly on the care of the wounded in the field. Henri Dunant's vision after Solferino had been simple: armies should be bound to pick up the fallen, no matter their uniform, and neutral volunteers should be permitted to help. That modest start expanded after the First World War, with the 1929 Geneva Convention on prisoners of war. The Second

World War, however, exposed the limits of these early treaties. Millions of prisoners perished in camps; civilians were starved, deported, and massacred. In 1949, the international community responded with the four Geneva Conventions still binding today: one for the wounded and sick on land, one for those shipwrecked at sea, one for prisoners of war, and one for civilians. Together with the 1977 Additional Protocols, they form the backbone of modern humanitarian law. Their rules are so widely accepted that the International Court of Justice has called them "intransgressible principles."

Beyond these foundational texts, treaties have emerged to address specific weapons or methods of war. The St. Petersburg Declaration of 1868 prohibited explosive projectiles under 400 grams, not because they were militarily ineffective, but because they inflicted needless suffering. The Hague Declaration of 1899 banned dum-dum bullets, whose mushrooming wounds were considered cruel. After the horrors of chemical warfare in the First World War, the Geneva Protocol of 1925 banned chemical and biological weapons. Later treaties went further: the Biological Weapons Convention of 1972 prohibited their development and stockpiling; the Chemical Weapons Convention of 1993 created an extensive verification regime. In the 1990s and 2000s, the Ottawa Treaty banning anti-personnel landmines and the Convention on Cluster Munitions outlawed weapons notorious for killing long after wars ended. And in 2017, the Treaty on the Prohibition of Nuclear Weapons sought to outlaw the most destructive arms of all, though the nuclear powers have so far refused to sign.

Each of these treaties represents both a recognition and a hope: recognition that war produces horrors, and hope that law can reduce them. They are imperfect — some states refuse to join, others join but violate — but their very existence creates standards against which conduct is measured. When a commander refrains from using a weapon, when a general staff cites proportionality, when a diplomat invokes Geneva, these texts live. They testify to the centuries-long struggle to discipline violence and to enshrine humanity even in humanity's darkest hour.

(PART 2)

As the 20th century dawned, the framework of humanitarian restraint seemed, at least on paper, to have achieved a measure of solidity. The Hague Conventions of 1899 and 1907 codified a wide range of principles: respect for family honor, protection of civilian property, humane treatment of prisoners, and prohibitions on certain weapons such as expanding bullets. Delegates at The Hague, drawn from across Europe, Asia, and the Americas, stood together to affirm that war, though brutal, must never be limitless. Yet in practice the very century that witnessed the most progress in writing down the law of war would also become the bloodiest stage of human history.

When the First World War broke out in 1914, the world was stunned by the sheer scale of destruction. Within weeks, armies numbering in the millions were grinding against each other along vast frontlines. Technology that had advanced faster than law or custom — machine guns, barbed wire, poison gas, and heavy artillery — reshaped the battlefield. The Hague prohibitions were put to the test, and in many cases, broken outright. The German use of chlorine gas at Ypres in 1915 violated the spirit of prior agreements against poison weapons, though defenders argued that because gas was not listed explicitly, it was not forbidden. The result was a cascade of escalation, as Britain and France developed their own chemical arsenals. By war's end, thousands lay dead or permanently blinded, scarred by gas that was supposed to be outside the pale of civilized conflict.

Still, even amid the carnage of the Western Front, the humanitarian instinct refused to vanish. The International Committee of the Red Cross organized prisoner-of-war visits, ensuring that captives were not wholly forgotten. Neutral states such as Switzerland served as intermediaries for POW mail and exchanges. Prisoner camps in some cases abided by standards that, however imperfect, drew directly from the Hague rules. Even trench warfare produced small moments of shared humanity — the Christmas Truce of 1914 being the most famous — when soldiers emerged from their trenches to exchange gifts and bury their dead, showing that the idea of restraint could flicker even in hellish conditions.

The shock of the First World War led to renewed attempts to reinforce and clarify the law. In 1925, the Geneva Protocol banned the use of chemical and biological weapons. Though not perfect — it did not forbid their development or stockpiling — the Protocol represented a collective cry of "never again." It was signed in the very city where Henri Dunant had launched the humanitarian revolution after Solferino, and its symbolic weight carried forward.

But the world had not learned enough. The Second World War erupted with even greater ferocity, testing the law of war to its limits. Nazi Germany's campaigns of terror, the Holocaust, Japan's atrocities in Nanking, and the devastation wrought by strategic bombing campaigns showed how fragile legal norms could be when states embraced ideology over humanity. Cities such as Dresden, Tokyo, and Hiroshima became synonymous with civilian suffering on a scale scarcely imaginable. Yet here too, law and conscience struggled to assert themselves.

The Geneva Conventions of 1929 had improved prisoner-of-war protections, and while violations abounded, they provided the basis for later accountability. The Nuremberg Trials after 1945 marked a turning point: for the first time, leaders were held criminally responsible for crimes against peace, war crimes, and crimes against humanity. Justice Robert Jackson, the American chief prosecutor, declared that Nuremberg was not "victors' justice," but an attempt to lay down principles for all future wars. The trials gave teeth to the law of war, transforming it from mere aspiration into enforceable obligation.

The horrors of the Second World War also spurred the revision and expansion of humanitarian law. In 1949, the Geneva Conventions were rewritten and strengthened. Now there were four distinct treaties: on the wounded and sick in the field, on the wounded and shipwrecked at sea, on prisoners of war, and on the protection of civilians. For the first time, civilians were not merely an implied concern but the central subject of an entire treaty. The Fourth Geneva Convention recognized that modern war would inevitably entangle whole populations, and therefore protections had to be explicit.

This expansion was not abstract; it was the world's response to actual suffering. Civilians who had been deported, starved, or massacred during the war became the silent witnesses behind the new articles. The memory of Anne Frank and millions like her haunted the negotiators. The phrase "never again," so often uttered after catastrophe, was translated into binding obligations.

The 1949 Conventions did more than add provisions; they established a framework for universality. Ratified by virtually every state on earth, they became the most widely accepted treaties in human history. They did not end atrocity, but they made clear that atrocity was unlawful. They created a moral baseline, a standard by which the world could measure conduct in war, and against which tribunals could later judge.

Yet the ink was scarcely dry before new conflicts arose — Korea, Algeria, Vietnam, and countless others — each testing whether the humanitarian promise could withstand the pressures of political necessity. Guerrilla warfare, insurgencies, and wars of decolonization posed new challenges: what happens when combatants do not wear uniforms, when civilians and fighters are intermingled? The law of war struggled to adapt. But through Additional Protocols in 1977, the Geneva framework reached further, extending protections to civilians in internal conflicts and clarifying the rules of distinction and proportionality.

The story of the law of war in the 20th century, then, is a story of both progress and tragedy. Every great violation produced not resignation but renewed resolve to codify protections more explicitly. At Ypres, gas introduced a new horror, and so came the Geneva Protocol. At Nanking, civilians suffered without recourse, and so came the Fourth Geneva Convention. At Auschwitz, the machinery of extermination shocked the conscience of humankind, and so came Nuremberg. The pattern was grim but real: atrocity, then law; suffering, then principle.

By the century's end, humanitarian law stood as one of the most developed and widely ratified branches of international law. But it remained fragile, dependent not only on treaties and conventions but on the will of soldiers, commanders, and states to honor their spirit. The 20th century revealed both the depths of cruelty and the stubborn endurance of conscience. In that tension lies the ongoing struggle that defines the law of war.

(PART 3)

If the 20th century forced the law of war to confront mechanized slaughter and genocide, the closing decades and the beginning of the 21st century challenged it with new kinds of conflict that blurred the line between war and peace. Civil wars, insurgencies, and terrorist campaigns complicated every assumption the earlier treaties had made about uniformed armies and declared wars. The rules were stretched, tested, and sometimes reinvented.

The Geneva Conventions had originally been written with interstate wars in mind — battles between sovereign nations with recognized armies. Yet by the 1960s and 1970s, most conflicts no longer looked like the Franco-Prussian War or the First World War. Instead, they were wars of decolonization, uprisings, and proxy wars within fragile states. Algeria's war for independence, for instance, was a brutal confrontation that showed how difficult it was to apply rules meant for armies to guerrillas and underground fighters. France insisted that the conflict was merely an internal matter and resisted granting prisoners the status of lawful combatants. Yet the international community increasingly demanded that captured insurgents be treated according to humanitarian standards, not merely as criminals.

Vietnam presented another test. American forces confronted an adversary — the Viet Cong — that blended into civilian populations, striking from villages and retreating into jungles. The principle of distinction — separating combatants from civilians — was pushed to its breaking point. Incidents such as the My Lai massacre in 1968, where hundreds of civilians were killed, became emblematic of the law's fragility in asymmetric conflict. Yet the outrage that followed also reinforced the need for clear rules and accountability. Courts-martial, investigative commissions, and a growing body of journalism made it impossible to claim that such acts were beyond the reach of law.

The challenge of irregular warfare led directly to the Additional Protocols of 1977, which supplemented the Geneva Conventions. Protocol I extended protections to civilians in international conflicts and clarified the prohibition on indiscriminate attacks. It explicitly recognized wars of national liberation as international conflicts, granting fighters in such wars combatant status if they carried arms openly before attacks and distinguished themselves from civilians when engaged. Protocol II, meanwhile, broke new ground by setting rules for non-international armed conflicts, where government forces and rebel groups fought within a single state. It outlawed attacks on civilians, emphasized humane treatment of all detainees, and banned collective punishment.

Though not universally ratified — the United States, for example, has not ratified Protocol I — the Additional Protocols represented an acknowledgment that war had changed, and law had to follow. They extended the humanitarian impulse into the messy terrain of civil war and insurgency, where the majority of modern victims were found.

At the same time, international justice expanded beyond the precedents of Nuremberg and Tokyo. For decades, the Cold War stalemate had prevented new tribunals. But in the 1990s, with the breakup of Yugoslavia and the genocide in Rwanda, the United Nations established ad hoc tribunals: the International Criminal Tribunal for the former Yugoslavia (ICTY) in 1993, and the International

Criminal Tribunal for Rwanda (ICTR) in 1994. These courts prosecuted crimes such as ethnic cleansing, mass rape, and genocide, holding both generals and politicians accountable.

The jurisprudence of these tribunals made history. In cases such as *Prosecutor v. Tadić* before the ICTY, the court confirmed that serious violations of humanitarian law applied not only in international wars but also in internal conflicts. The ICTR's landmark decision in *Prosecutor v. Akayesu* recognized rape as a constitutive act of genocide, forever altering how international law understood sexual violence in war. These decisions did not merely punish; they clarified and expanded the content of humanitarian law, showing that it was alive, not fossilized.

Building on these tribunals, the international community created the International Criminal Court (ICC) in 1998 through the Rome Statute. Unlike Nuremberg or the ICTY, the ICC was not a temporary response to a specific war but a permanent court with global jurisdiction over genocide, crimes against humanity, war crimes, and aggression. Its establishment was hailed as a milestone, though its reach has been contested by powerful states that refuse membership. Still, the ICC embodies the ambition that no one, no matter how high their office, is above the law of war.

The turn of the 21st century brought new challenges: the global war on terror, the rise of non-state armed groups like al-Qaeda and ISIS, and the increased use of drones and cyber operations. After the attacks of September 11, 2001, the United States launched military operations in Afghanistan and later Iraq. But in both wars, questions arose about detention, interrogation, and targeting. The Bush administration's creation of the detention camp at Guantánamo Bay raised fierce debates about whether captured fighters were prisoners of war or "unlawful combatants." The use of "enhanced interrogation techniques," widely regarded as torture, drew condemnation from human rights organizations and reaffirmed the importance of the Convention Against Torture and Common Article 3 of the Geneva Conventions.

Meanwhile, drone warfare complicated traditional notions of battlefield and combatant. When missiles were fired at suspected militants in Pakistan or Yemen, often far from declared battlefields, critics asked whether the strikes complied with the principles of distinction and proportionality. Could the law of war stretch to cover remote-controlled weapons and global surveillance, or was a new framework needed? The debates continue, but what is clear is that the humanitarian principles remain as relevant as ever: civilians must be spared, force must be proportionate, and dignity must be preserved.

Even cyberspace has entered the conversation. States now debate whether cyber operations that disable infrastructure — say, a hospital network or a power grid — amount to attacks under humanitarian law. The Tallinn Manual, produced by a group of experts in 2013, applied existing law of war principles to cyber operations, suggesting that the Geneva Conventions are robust enough to cover new domains.

Through all these developments, one lesson recurs: the law of war is not static. It is dynamic, responding to new forms of violence while clinging to old principles. The instinct that drove Cicero to say "even war has its laws," that inspired Dunant after Solferino, that carried into the Geneva Conventions and Nuremberg, is the same instinct at work in today's debates over drones and cyberattacks. The tools change, but the question remains constant: how to preserve humanity in the midst of inhumanity.

CHAPTER 4

FROM CATASTROPHE TO LAW (PART 1)

The First and Second World Wars were not only cataclysms of violence; they were also crucibles that reshaped the very fabric of the law of war. Out of their ruins came some of the most important treaties, institutions, and precedents we still rely on today. The nineteenth-century rules, from the Lieber Instructions to the Hague Conventions, had laid down the principle that war should be limited. But the world wars demonstrated how fragile those limits could be, and how urgently they needed reinforcement.

The First World War tested humanitarian law in ways that no earlier conflict had. Machine guns, poison gas, and long-range artillery created a scale of killing that shocked even seasoned commanders. The Hague Conventions of 1899 and 1907 had already prohibited certain weapons, such as poison gas and expanding bullets, yet on the Western Front, chlorine, phosgene, and mustard gas were unleashed in disregard of these prohibitions. The horror of gas attacks, with soldiers blinded and lungs destroyed, seared itself into memory and shaped future prohibitions.

Prisoners of war were taken in enormous numbers during the war, and here the law showed both strength and weakness. The 1907 Hague Convention required humane treatment, but enforcement was uneven. In some camps, prisoners received adequate food and medical care; in others, they starved or labored under brutal conditions. The International Committee of the Red Cross (ICRC), founded in the wake of Henri Dunant's appeal after Solferino, intervened tirelessly, visiting camps, delivering mail, and pressing governments to comply with their obligations. Its work during the First World War elevated its status as the neutral guardian of humanitarian law.

The Second World War was worse. Entire populations were uprooted, starved, or exterminated. The deliberate targeting of civilians reached a scale that overwhelmed earlier conventions. The bombing of Guernica in 1937 by German and Italian aircraft during the Spanish Civil War foreshadowed what would come. By 1945, the aerial bombardments of London, Dresden, Tokyo, Hiroshima, and Nagasaki revealed the terrifying consequences of strategic bombing campaigns. Civilian immunity, a cornerstone of humanitarian law, had been shattered.

The Holocaust represented not just a violation of law but a descent into barbarism that forced a complete rethinking of what law could do. Six million Jews, along with Romani people, disabled persons, political dissidents, and others, were systematically exterminated. The Nazi regime not only trampled the Hague and Geneva rules but obliterated the very idea that law might restrain war. It took the shock of Auschwitz, Bergen-Belsen, and Treblinka to galvanize the world into crafting stronger safeguards.

The Nuremberg Trials, held from 1945 to 1946, were the most visible attempt to restore law's authority. For the first time, leaders were prosecuted not just for waging aggressive war but for crimes against humanity. Figures such as Hermann Göring, Rudolf Hess, and Joachim von Ribbentrop stood in the dock, charged with planning wars of aggression, orchestrating atrocities, and annihilating civilian populations. The tribunal rejected the defense of "just following orders" and insisted that individuals — even heads of state — bore personal responsibility for violations of the law of war. Twelve were sentenced to death, seven to prison, and three were acquitted.

The Tokyo Tribunal followed, holding Japanese leaders accountable for atrocities in Asia and the Pacific, including the Rape of Nanking and the abuse of prisoners of war. General Hideki Tojo, Japan's former prime minister, was among those sentenced to death. Both Nuremberg and Tokyo established the precedent that accountability could reach beyond national borders, that the international community had authority to judge crimes of war and crimes against humanity.

From the ashes of these conflicts emerged the 1949 Geneva Conventions, the most comprehensive codification of humanitarian law in history. The first three conventions revised earlier treaties on wounded soldiers and prisoners of war, while the fourth — entirely new — focused on civilians in occupied territories. It prohibited deportations, collective punishments, and reprisals against civilians. It insisted that occupying powers had duties to maintain order and provide for the population. For the first time, civilian protection was recognized as equal in importance to the protection of soldiers.

These follow closely the 1948 Convention on the Prevention and Punishment of the Crime of Genocide, spurred by Raphael Lemkin, who coined the very word "genocide." It declared genocide a crime under international law, binding states to prevent and punish it. While political realities would later delay enforcement, the Genocide Convention reflected a determination that Auschwitz should never be repeated.

These postwar instruments did not eliminate atrocity, but they gave the world a yardstick against which to measure behavior, a vocabulary of accountability, and a promise of dignity even amid war.

(PART 2)

The Geneva Conventions of 1949 were the starting point, but not the endpoint. Wars of decolonization, superpower conflicts, and insurgencies soon revealed gaps in the law. The challenge of occupation stood out most clearly. After the Second World War, Allied forces occupied Germany and Japan. Unlike earlier occupations that often sought annexation or plunder, these occupations aimed to rebuild, democratize, and eventually return sovereignty. Yet they also demonstrated the tension between the occupier's duty to maintain order and the temptation to reshape societies according to its own ideals.

Occupation law is, at its core, a compromise. It insists that the occupier is not sovereign, but only a temporary administrator. It requires the occupier to respect local laws and institutions unless absolutely prevented, to maintain order and provide for the population, and to safeguard cultural property and religious practice. At the same time, it demands that the occupied population not resist violently once effective control has been established. This uneasy balance between protector and controller continues to challenge both occupiers and occupied.

In practice, violations have been common. During the Second World War, German occupation policies across Europe deliberately flouted the Hague and Geneva rules. Civilians were deported for forced labor, food supplies were confiscated, and reprisals for resistance were brutal. The deportation of Jews from occupied Poland and France to extermination camps represented the absolute negation of occupation law's protective purpose. After the war, these acts became a core focus at Nuremberg.

Later conflicts tested the rules anew. The Israeli occupation of Palestinian territories after 1967 raised ongoing questions about settlement activity, the treatment of detainees, and the responsibilities of an occupying power. The United States' occupation of Iraq in 2003 provided another test case, where the Coalition Provisional Authority faced criticism for dismantling Iraqi institutions in ways many argued contravened the occupier's duty to preserve the existing civic structure. Each of these examples underscored that occupation law was not an academic curiosity, but a daily question of governance, rights, and survival.

The 1977 Additional Protocols to the Geneva Conventions extended these protections. Protocol I clarified the obligations of occupying powers, while Protocol II addressed non-international armed conflicts — civil wars, insurgencies, and other internal struggles that had become the dominant form of warfare in the modern era. These protocols reaffirmed the core humanitarian imperatives: no targeting civilians, no use of starvation as a method of warfare, no destruction of cultural heritage.

Accountability, however, remained uneven. While Nuremberg and Tokyo had held leaders to account, the Cold War stymied many efforts to enforce the law of war. Atrocities in Vietnam, Algeria, and elsewhere often went unpunished on the international stage, even when documented by journalists, NGOs, and independent commissions. It took the post–Cold War era to revive the project of international justice.

In the 1990s, the world saw the establishment of ad hoc tribunals that brought occupation and civilian protection back to the center. The International Criminal Tribunal for the former Yugoslavia (ICTY) prosecuted leaders for ethnic cleansing, mass rape, and the deliberate shelling of cities. Slobodan Milošević, the former president of Serbia, became the first head of state indicted by an international tribunal while still in power. Although he died in 2006 before a verdict could be reached, his trial demonstrated that sovereignty was no longer a shield against accountability.

The International Criminal Tribunal for Rwanda (ICTR) likewise addressed atrocities in which occupation and control were wielded to facilitate genocide. Jean Kambanda, the Rwandan prime minister during the genocide, pled guilty to genocide and was sentenced to life in prison — the first such sentence handed down by an international court. His conviction underscored that political leadership carried direct responsibility for the crimes committed under their governance.

Out of these tribunals grew the permanent International Criminal Court (ICC), established by the Rome Statute in 1998. The ICC asserted jurisdiction over war crimes, crimes against humanity, genocide, and the crime of aggression. Though not universally accepted — with some major powers refusing to join — the ICC represented a culmination of the long struggle to enforce humanitarian norms.

The law of occupation, then, is not a relic of the nineteenth century but a living framework. It is a reminder that conquest has been disavowed, annexation forbidden, and that occupation is always temporary. More importantly, it is a moral insistence that when one society falls under the control of another, the conqueror becomes responsible not only for its own actions but for the dignity, survival, and humanity of those under its control.

Chapter 5

The Conduct of Hostilities (Part 1)

The law of war lives most vividly in the crucible of battle, where principles must be tested against urgent military necessity. The conduct of hostilities — the way armies engage with each other — is where humanity and necessity collide most directly. Commanders and soldiers stand at the crossroads: their choices in targeting, weaponry, and tactics determine whether the restraints of law survive or shatter under pressure.

One of the central principles guiding the conduct of hostilities is distinction: the obligation to distinguish between combatants and civilians. This rule sounds simple, yet it has been among the most difficult to enforce in modern conflicts. In the trench battles of the First World War, the distinction was relatively straightforward — opposing armies wore uniforms, faced each other across no man's land, and civilians were largely removed from the immediate front lines. But by the Second World War, and especially in later conflicts such as Vietnam, Algeria, or Afghanistan, the boundaries blurred. Insurgents dressed as civilians, civilians carried food or weapons to fighters, and combat zones spread into villages and cities.

The prohibition against indiscriminate attacks arose precisely because of these challenges. The bombing of Guernica in 1937, immortalized in Picasso's painting, showed the horror of targeting a civilian town for psychological effect. The indiscriminate bombardment of London during the Blitz, and later the firebombing of Dresden and Tokyo, took this logic to its extreme. Whole cities were transformed into ash and rubble, with tens of thousands killed in a single night. Even if military targets were present, the destruction was far beyond what distinction or proportionality would allow.

Proportionality itself remains a vexed concept. The rule is simple: an attack is prohibited if the expected civilian harm is excessive in relation to the anticipated military advantage. But how should commanders weigh a destroyed tank against a school full of children? In practice, proportionality requires judgment, sometimes under fire, with imperfect information. Courts and tribunals have recognized this tension. In the aftermath of NATO's intervention in Kosovo in 1999, for example, questions were raised about the bombing of a Serbian television station, which killed civilian staff. NATO argued it was a legitimate command-and-control target, while critics called it a war crime. The International Criminal Tribunal for the former Yugoslavia (ICTY) ultimately declined to prosecute, but the case highlighted the fragile balance inherent in proportionality assessments.

Another rule central to hostilities is the prohibition of perfidy — acts that betray the enemy's trust in order to kill or wound. Feigning surrender, misuse of protective symbols like the Red Cross, or pretending to be a civilian to ambush soldiers all fall into this category. Perfidy corrodes the basic trust that makes humanitarian law workable. If soldiers cannot believe a white flag, then surrender becomes impossible, and wars descend into slaughter without quarter. The Lieber Instructions of 1863, already familiar with the brutality of the American Civil War, condemned perfidy explicitly, and the prohibition has echoed through subsequent treaties.

Similarly, the rule against denying quarter — refusing to spare the life of an enemy who surrenders — stands as a bedrock of the law of war. To kill those who have laid down arms is not only unlawful but destructive of any chance at reconciliation. History is filled with massacres where quarter was denied, from medieval sackings of cities to the killing of prisoners at Malmedy during the Battle of the Bulge in 1944. Each such episode reaffirmed why the rule must be absolute: to accept surrender is to accept the possibility of an end to killing.

Weapons too fall within the law's concern over hostilities. Expanding bullets, designed to cause grievous wounds, were banned as early as the 1899 Hague Declaration. Chemical weapons, their horror evident at Ypres in 1915, were outlawed by the 1925 Geneva Protocol. Yet violations recurred: mustard gas in the Ethiopian war of 1935, nerve agents in the Iran–Iraq conflict of the 1980s, chlorine and sarin in the Syrian civil war. Each violation reignited the debate over deterrence and accountability.

In modern times, the use of drones and precision-guided munitions has been defended as a way to minimize collateral damage. Yet drone warfare raises new questions: what about targeting individuals far from a battlefield, or the psychological toll on civilian populations living under the constant hum of surveillance?

Here again, distinction and proportionality are tested in evolving contexts.

Underlying all of this is the tension between military necessity and humanitarian restraint. Military necessity permits what is necessary to defeat the enemy, but not what is cruel, wanton, or excessive. Humanity requires mercy, protection, and limits even in war. The law of hostilities, then, is an attempt to reconcile these imperatives: to allow armies to fight, but to insist that they fight within boundaries that preserve a space for humanity to endure.

(PART 2)

One of the most controversial aspects of the conduct of hostilities has been reprisals — acts that would otherwise be unlawful, carried out in retaliation with the hope of deterring the enemy. In earlier centuries, reprisals were accepted as a grim part of war. If one side executed prisoners, the other might retaliate by threatening the same. Yet the modern law of war has steadily narrowed their legitimacy. The Hague Conventions permitted reprisals only under strict conditions, and the Geneva Conventions of 1949 prohibited reprisals against protected persons — meaning civilians, prisoners of war, and the wounded. The reasoning is simple: vengeance against the vulnerable is never justified. Still, reprisals against combatants remain a gray area, and the temptation to escalate remains strong.

Siege warfare has long been one of the harshest features of battle. From medieval castles starved into submission to modern cities encircled by artillery, sieges test the limits of endurance and humanity. The law permits siege as a method of warfare, but forbids starvation of civilians as a means of attack. The Additional Protocol I of 1977 made this explicit, declaring starvation of civilians unlawful. Yet the rule has often been ignored. In Leningrad during the Second World War, over a million civilians died as German forces choked off food and supplies. More recently, in the Syrian civil war, besieged cities like Aleppo and Eastern Ghouta suffered deliberate denial of food and medicine, in defiance of international law. These episodes illustrate both the endurance of siege as a tactic and the difficulty of enforcing humanitarian limits in the face of military desperation.

Urban warfare compounds these dilemmas. Modern battles are increasingly fought in cities, where civilians and combatants live side by side. The destruction of Grozny during the Chechen wars, the battles of Fallujah in Iraq, and the ongoing devastation of cities in Ukraine all reveal the immense challenges of applying distinction and proportionality in dense urban environments. Apartment buildings may conceal snipers, hospitals may be commandeered as bases, and civilian neighborhoods may sit atop underground bunkers. Commanders must make rapid choices with devastating consequences, balancing military gain against the certainty of civilian loss.

The use of civilians as shields represents one of the most egregious violations of the law of hostilities. When combatants deliberately place military assets in or near schools, hospitals, or monuments, they endanger those very sites and people. The Hague and Geneva rules, as well as subsequent protocols, prohibit such tactics. Yet the practice has persisted. In the wars in Gaza, accusations of human shields have been leveled repeatedly, fueling debate about responsibility when civilians die in such contexts. The law remains clear: the presence of civilians does not nullify the attacker's obligations of proportionality and precaution.

Starvation as a method of warfare is another tactic the law has tried to abolish. Article 54 of Protocol I forbids attacks on "objects indispensable to the survival of the civilian population," such as food, crops, and water supplies. Yet famine has been used as a weapon in conflicts from Biafra in the late 1960s to Yemen in recent years. When food is denied, it is the most vulnerable — children, the elderly, the poor — who suffer first and most severely. The law's prohibition is absolute, but the gap between principle and practice is wide.

Technology has added another layer to the conduct of hostilities. Cyber operations, though not yet fully addressed in treaties, raise questions familiar from earlier ages: can power grids, water systems, or hospitals be targeted digitally? If a cyberattack disables civilian infrastructure, causing harm without firing a shot, is it different from dropping bombs? The Tallinn Manual, produced by legal experts, has tried to apply the principles of distinction, proportionality, and necessity to cyberspace. But without binding treaties, these issues remain unsettled, a new frontier in the law of hostilities.

Despite these challenges, the law of hostilities serves as a compass. It cannot eliminate suffering, but it can orient choices. When commanders refrain from bombing a city market, when soldiers accept an enemy's surrender, when armies allow humanitarian corridors, they act in the spirit of the law. Each restraint, however small, affirms that war is not a license for cruelty without limit.

CHAPTER 6

WEAPONS: WHAT CAN AND CANNOT BE USED (PART 1)

Weapons are the grammar of war: they shape how a conflict speaks and what it says about the parties who fight. The law of war does not pretend that weapons are neutral; it insists that some means of wounding and killing are too cruel, too indiscriminate, or too long-lasting in their harm to be acceptable. The rule that runs through every prohibition is simple to state and hard to apply: do not use means or methods of warfare that cause superfluous injury or unnecessary suffering, and do not employ weapons that cannot be directed at a specific military objective. From the soft-point "dum-dum" bullet of a century ago to the possibility of autonomous machines deciding life and death today, the argument has always been the same — humanity must restrain its tools even as it seeks advantage.

The earliest modern example of legal restraint on weapons is eloquent in its modesty. The St.

Petersburg Declaration of 1868 focused narrowly on explosive projectiles below a certain size, but its principle was sweeping: it banned weapons that produced suffering disproportionate to any military advantage they might bring. That sentiment found immediate expression in the Hague conferences that followed. In 1899 the use of expanding bullets — the so-called dum-dums that mushroom in flesh and produced horrific wounds — was forbidden. The underlying concern was not mere squeamishness: wounds that shatter tissue, cause irreversible infection, or produce prolonged agony for no added military benefit were judged morally and legally unacceptable. The prohibition of such bullets is one of the clearest early instances where law tried to constrict what combatants may use against each other.

World War I forced a far harsher reckoning. The introduction of chemical agents — chlorine, phosgene, and later mustard gas — changed battlefields from places of mortal risk into scenes of grotesque suffering. Soldiers blinded, choked, and burned; victims were often left with lifelong injuries. International revulsion produced the 1925 Geneva

Protocol, which forbade the use of chemical and biological agents in war. The Protocol did not immediately stop development or stockpiling — states continued research and, in some cases, use — but it placed chemical and biological weapons on the list of tools that civilized states should not employ. When Iran used mustard and nerve agents in the 1980s against Iraqi Kurds and on the battlefield, the outrage confirmed that treaty words matter; violations generate diplomatic, moral, and sometimes criminal consequences.

Nuclear weapons present the law of weapons with its most difficult moral and legal problem. The atomic bombings of Hiroshima and Nagasaki in August 1945 exposed a scale of destruction whose effects were not momentary but multigenerational: heat, blast, and radiation combined to kill and maim, to destroy cities, and to poison environments for decades. The question that followed — can any legal system permit the use of weapons that so blatantly violate distinction and proportionality — has never been fully answered. The International Court of Justice, in an advisory opinion in 1996, concluded that the use of nuclear weapons would generally be contrary to the principles of humanitarian law, though it left open an uncertain narrow circumstance of extreme self-defense where lawful use could not be definitively excluded. Politically, many states sought a complete ban; legally and strategically, nuclear deterrence kept those most able to outlaw them from joining prohibition treaties. The Treaty on the Prohibition of Nuclear Weapons (2017) represents the moral and political impulse to ban such arms; its limited membership shows the persistent tension between law, conscience, and perceived security.

Some weapons cause harm long after the guns fall silent. Anti-personnel landmines and cluster munitions are notorious for this. Mines are cheap, easily distributed, and effective in denying territory — which explains their appeal — yet they remain in the ground for decades, maiming farmers, children, and returning refugees. The Ottawa Treaty (1997) banned antipersonnel mines and established an international program of clearance and victim assistance; states party to the treaty have destroyed millions of stockpiled mines and funded clearance programs. Cluster munitions scatter bomblets over wide areas; many fail to detonate on impact, becoming de facto landmines. The Convention on Cluster Munitions (2008) responded to the civilian suffering these weapons caused. The legal judgments that produced these treaties were rooted in the simple observation that weapons whose effects cannot be limited to a military moment are intolerable for civilians living in war's aftermath.

The rules against certain weapons are also instruments of moral pedagogy. When states outlaw expanding bullets, chemical agents, landmines, or cluster munitions, they do something more than change tactics: they shape the way soldiers and societies imagine warfare. Weapons law inculcates a sense of restraint. Manuals and training emphasize that legality is not an abstract lecture but a rule of life for the armed person: what you may aim at, what you may fire, and what you must refuse to use.

Yet prohibitions are only as strong as enforcement and the willingness of states to adopt them. Chemical weapons persisted after 1925; mines remained ubiquitous into the 1990s; cluster munitions were used in conflicts even after some states agreed to the convention. Each violation has been met with condemnation and (sometimes) with sanctions, but the pattern is sobering. Law can shape behavior, but it cannot, by itself, end the temptation to exploit cruel or convenient weapons when stakes are thought to justify them.

A further category of restriction concerns means rather than specific munitions. The law forbids use of weapons that are inherently indiscriminate — that is, weapons that cannot be directed against a military objective or whose effects cannot be limited. Indiscriminate weapons make distinction impossible: if there is no way to aim only at soldiers and not at a civilian market, their use is outlawed. This legal logic underlies campaigns against area bombardment of cities and motivated the measures against landmines and cluster munitions. New technologies complicate this calculus. GPS-guided munitions and precision weapons promise to reduce collateral harm; but their precision can be illusory — the intelligence feeding targeting decisions may be flawed, or a building that was thought to be empty may harbor civilians. The law therefore demands precautions and verification: feasible steps to confirm targets, warnings where possible, and cancellation of attacks when doubt remains.

Modern debates about weapons have moved into even newer territory. Two issues have dominated recent discussion: autonomous weapons systems and cyber operations. Autonomous weapons, sometimes dubbed "killer robots," raise a foundational question: can machines be permitted to choose to take life? Many scholars and practitioners argue that human judgment — with its capacity for moral assessment, proportionality balancing, and empathy — cannot be displaced by algorithms. Others contend that autonomous systems could, if properly constrained, reduce civilian casualties by reacting faster and more precisely than human operators. The legal community has not reached consensus; some states and NGOs press for preventive bans, others for strict regulation and "meaningful human control" over any lethal use.

Cyber operations complicate weapon law because they do not always leave visible scars. A malware attack on a hospital information system can disable life-saving equipment, isolate patients from monitoring, and indirectly cause deaths. If a cyberattack disables a city's power grid in winter, resulting in casualties from cold or lack of medical care, is that functionally indistinguishable from bombing a city's power plant? The Tallinn Manual and related expert work have sought to apply existing principles — distinction, proportionality, and necessity — to cyber operations, but the rapid pace of technological change and the difficulty of attribution make the field legally unsettled.

Finally, the law addresses munitions and ammunition designed to inflict cruel wounds. The long-standing ban on expanding bullets remains salient: hollow-point and soft-point bullets that mushroom inside tissue are unlawful in international armed conflict when used against combatants, on the theory that they cause unnecessary suffering without commensurate military advantage. Similarly, explosive projectiles intended to fragment and cause maximum tissue damage in small arms are suspect. These rules aim not to reduce the lethality of combatants per se but to prevent wounds that produce prolonged agony or suffering out of proportion to the military advantage obtained.

The trajectory of weapons law reveals an underlying ethic: as weapons become more destructive or more indiscriminate, the legal and moral pressure to restrain their use intensifies. That ethic is not purely idealistic. It is practical: weapons that outrage audiences, leave long-term humanitarian crises, and provoke legal condemnation tend to cost the user politically and strategically. Soldiers trained to respect limits are more likely to take surrender and to preserve post-conflict order. Nations that build norms against the cruelest means of violence create a space in which postwar reconciliation is possible.

In short, weapons law attempts to answer a stark question: if we must hurt and kill, how can we do so without obliterating the conditions of human dignity that make life worth reclaiming after the fighting stops? The answers are imperfect and contested, but they exist. They are treaties, doctrines, manuals, and — crucially — the moral judgments of commanders who must decide in the moment whether a means is necessary and whether it crosses the line into needless suffering.

(PART 2)

Rules about weapons would mean little if they were never enforced. The history of modern warfare shows repeated violations, but also moments when the international community, through outrage or judicial process, responded in ways that strengthened the prohibitions. These responses remind us that the law of war is not static; it adapts, sometimes painfully, as weapons evolve and as conscience sharpens.

The First World War's use of poison gas is the classic example. The Hague Conventions had already banned chemical agents, but by 1915, clouds of chlorine rolled across the trenches at Ypres. The devastation was immediate — soldiers died in convulsions, and survivors carried scars for life. After the war, the world reaffirmed the ban through the 1925 Geneva Protocol. For decades, major powers kept chemical weapons in storage, often rationalizing that deterrence required possession even if use was forbidden. It took the Iran–Iraq War of the 1980s, with Saddam Hussein's forces gassing both Iranian troops and Kurdish civilians, to remind the world that prohibition without accountability is hollow. The outrage helped build momentum for the Chemical Weapons Convention of 1993, which not only banned use but required destruction of stockpiles under international verification.

The use of landmines offers another story of prohibition through persistence. By the 1990s, reports of children maimed in Cambodia, Angola, and Afghanistan galvanized public opinion. The International Campaign to Ban Landmines, led by Jody Williams, harnessed grassroots activism into a global treaty. The 1997 Ottawa Treaty banned anti-personnel mines outright. Over 160 states have since joined, and millions of mines have been destroyed. Yet key military powers remain outside, citing tactical utility. The tension illustrates the law's challenge: norms can grow strong even without universal membership, but their ultimate effectiveness depends on whether the most capable users submit.

Cluster munitions drew similar condemnation after widespread use in Lebanon in 2006. Human Rights Watch and other NGOs documented unexploded bomblets littering fields, homes, and playgrounds. In response, the 2008 Convention on Cluster Munitions outlawed their use, stockpiling, and transfer. The treaty has saved lives through clearance programs, yet once again, some major states declined to join. Still, even non-parties often feel the stigma: their use is condemned as an outlier, a violation of humanitarian conscience, even if not formally illegal under the treaty for those states.

Tribunals have occasionally addressed weapons directly. The ICTY, in its jurisprudence, ruled that the use of certain methods — such as shelling civilian areas indiscriminately — could itself constitute unlawful weapon use. While no international court has yet prosecuted individuals specifically for employing landmines or cluster munitions, the principle is clear: commanders may be held accountable for authorizing weapons that are inherently indiscriminate or cause unnecessary suffering.

The rise of nuclear weapons introduced a different dynamic. Unlike landmines or cluster munitions, nuclear arsenals remain central to the security doctrines of major powers. The Treaty on the Non-Proliferation of Nuclear Weapons (NPT), signed in 1968, sought to prevent new states from acquiring them while gradually reducing the stockpiles of those that had them. Yet disarmament has been halting. The 2017 Treaty on the Prohibition of Nuclear Weapons expressed the conscience of much of the international community, declaring the weapons unlawful in every respect. Nuclear-armed states, however, have refused to sign. The law here rests less on treaty compliance than on moral stigma and political pressure, which nonetheless shape debates on deterrence and legitimacy.

In the present, the conversations about autonomous weapons and cyber warfare are shaped not only by fear but also by anticipation. Unlike landmines, which had decades of carnage before prohibition, autonomous systems may be constrained before they see widespread use. Campaigns like "Stop Killer Robots" echo the landmine movement, aiming to stigmatize before proliferation. Cyber operations are more complex: states are reluctant to bind themselves, yet even here the principle is recognized — if a cyberattack kills civilians by knocking out a hospital's power, the law of war has been breached.

The enduring lesson of weapons law is that each generation faces the temptation to create new means of destruction. Some will always argue that restraint weakens military strength. Yet history shows that when weapons provoke horror, when their use scars societies for generations, law eventually rises to meet the challenge.

Each prohibition is not only a legal rule but a memory made permanent: a reminder that humanity recoiled, and chose to draw a line.

CHAPTER 7

PRISONERS OF WAR (PART 1)

The treatment of prisoners has always revealed a society's true measure of humanity, or its lack. From the earliest empires of the ancient Near East to the muddy trenches of the First World War, captives have been at once symbols of triumph and tests of conscience. Their fate tells us much about whether restraint is possible in the face of victory's intoxication.

In antiquity, restraint was rare. The Assyrian kings boasted in stone inscriptions of chaining enemies, blinding them, or parading them like trophies. Their art depicts prisoners led by hooks through their lips, an image of utter degradation. Persia offered a partial contrast. Cyrus the Great, when he conquered Babylon in 539 BCE, proclaimed that he would not enslave the population or destroy their temples. His "Cyrus Cylinder," often called the first declaration of human rights, may not have been as pure as it sounds — but it shows the tension between cruelty and clemency even then.

China's dynasties oscillated between brutality and pragmatism. Some emperors executed captives en masse to terrify rivals, while others absorbed them into the empire's bureaucracy or armies. The Qin, famous for harsh discipline, buried alive thousands of surrendered soldiers. Later dynasties, especially the Tang, sometimes offered captured enemies a role within their own military structures — a recognition that humanity and utility could align.

The Greeks, too, wrestled with the problem. In Homer's *Iliad*, Hector imagines his wife enslaved if Troy should fall, and Achilles slaughters captives at Patroclus' funeral pyre. Yet the Greeks also developed the practice of ransoming high-born prisoners, preserving their lives in exchange for wealth. The Athenians, more unusually, sometimes granted prisoners of war the right to live as "metics" — resident foreigners. This mingling of cruelty and mercy ran through their culture.

Rome institutionalized both. Prisoners were paraded in triumphs, sometimes strangled at the end of the spectacle. Yet many were sold into slavery rather than killed, a pragmatic acknowledgment of their value as labor. Over time, Rome also recognized the inviolability of ambassadors and heralds, planting an early seed of what would later become diplomatic immunity. Even in its ruthlessness, Rome occasionally glimpsed the necessity of restraint.

The medieval world shifted toward ransom as a system. Knights captured in battle were often worth more alive than dead. At Agincourt in 1415, Henry V initially ordered the killing of French prisoners, fearing they might overwhelm his reduced force if they rose up. Chroniclers recorded this order with unease, for by then the ransom economy had embedded the idea that prisoners ought to be spared. The value of a captive was no longer only symbolic but financial — a development that, ironically, fostered humanitarian restraint.

Naval warfare brought its own customs. Shipwrecked sailors, even enemies, were often rescued by those who had sunk their vessels. Sometimes this mercy was practical — a sailor might be exchanged later — but sometimes it was simply solidarity among men who knew the sea could claim anyone without warning. Already, the shared dangers of a profession softened enmity.

The early modern period witnessed attempts to codify better standards. Hugo Grotius, writing in *De Jure Belli ac Pacis* (1625), argued that prisoners should not be slaughtered, for once disarmed they no longer posed a threat. His logic was not sentimental but rational: necessity could not justify cruelty beyond what military advantage required. Grotius was not alone. Alberico Gentili, a century earlier, had urged that the lives of captives should be spared whenever possible. These thinkers marked the beginning of a legal discourse on prisoners that would bear fruit centuries later.

The Thirty Years' War (1618–1648) tested these ideals. Massacres of prisoners occurred, but sometimes restraint prevailed. The Treaty of Westphalia in 1648 implicitly recognized that prisoners should be exchanged or released rather than exterminated, a recognition born of exhaustion after decades of carnage. By the eighteenth century, more formalized exchanges developed, particularly in conflicts between European powers. Officers were often paroled — allowed to return home on their promise not to rejoin the fight until formally exchanged. This practice blended honor with law, showing that the notion of parole had become a recognized institution.

When the American Revolution erupted, the issue arose anew. The British at first refused to treat captured Americans as legitimate combatants, viewing them as rebels and traitors. George Washington protested vigorously, insisting that his men were lawful prisoners of war entitled to humane treatment. He threatened retaliation if they were mistreated, a strategy that eventually compelled the British to shift their stance. Already, the reciprocity principle — "treat ours well, or yours will suffer" — was a crude but effective enforcement mechanism.

The Napoleonic Wars saw prisoner populations swell into the tens of thousands. Camps were established in Britain and France, some reasonably humane, others less so. In Britain, Norman Cross became a vast camp where prisoners built models, wrote diaries, and survived years of captivity. These experiences left behind records that influenced later thinking on humanitarian standards. They also revealed how fragile those standards could be: shortages of food, outbreaks of disease, and the temptations of cruelty all pushed camps toward suffering.

By the nineteenth century, the idea of regulating captivity gained momentum. The Lieber Instructions of 1863, issued during the American Civil War, forbade cruelty toward prisoners and insisted they be treated humanely, though they could be confined until exchanged. Lieber declared that "military necessity does not admit of cruelty" — a principle that echoed forward into Hague and Geneva law. His code banned summary executions and insisted that prisoners must not be subjected to revenge.

World War I put these ideas to the test on an unprecedented scale. Millions of prisoners filled camps across Europe. Some were treated decently; others languished in squalor. The International Committee of the Red Cross, founded half a century earlier, stepped into this crisis by visiting camps, delivering relief parcels, and serving as a conduit for communication between captives and their families. Its role as neutral guardian became entrenched. Yet the suffering was still immense: Russian prisoners in Germany and Austria endured freezing conditions and food shortages, while German prisoners in

France and Britain sometimes faced forced labor under harsh discipline. Disease claimed thousands. Still, compared to earlier centuries, the survival of millions of POWs testified to how far the idea of humanitarian law had progressed.

Stories from the war bring this home. At one camp in Switzerland, severely wounded prisoners from both sides were exchanged and allowed to convalesce in the neutral country, surrounded by alpine air rather than barbed wire. Letters survive of French and German soldiers alike describing their gratitude at being spared death by neglect. These glimpses of humanity, amid a war otherwise so mechanized and merciless, remind us why law matters: it preserves the possibility of dignity even for the defeated.

Thus, by the eve of World War II, the framework for POW protection was already established. Ransom and parole had faded, replaced by codified rules. The Hague Regulations of 1907 required humane treatment of captives. The Geneva Convention of 1929 expanded these protections further, mandating standards for food, labor, and correspondence. It was imperfect, but it represented a collective commitment that prisoners of war must not be left to the whims of vengeance. The foundation had been laid, though it would be tested to its breaking point in the next global conflict.

Prisoners of War (Part 2)

The Second World War shattered any illusions that the framework for protecting prisoners was secure. The Geneva Convention of 1929, signed by most major powers, set forth obligations for humane treatment, but its reach was uneven and its observance inconsistent. The vast scale of the conflict meant that millions fell into captivity, and their fate varied dramatically depending on who held them.

On the Eastern Front, the law of war all but collapsed. The German Wehrmacht, acting under Nazi ideology, treated captured Soviet soldiers as subhuman. Millions were marched into camps without shelter, starved, or executed outright. Historians estimate that more than three million Soviet prisoners died in German hands. The Germans refused to extend Geneva protections to them, arguing that the Soviet Union had not ratified the 1929 Convention. This was a legal fig leaf for deliberate extermination, part of a larger war of annihilation. Conversely, Soviet treatment of German captives was harsh, involving forced labor in mines and forests, with high mortality rates, though not on the genocidal scale seen in German policy.

Elsewhere, practices varied. In the Pacific theater, Japanese forces often ignored international law altogether. The infamous Bataan Death March in 1942 saw thousands of American and Filipino prisoners beaten, deprived of food and water, and executed along the route. Allied prisoners forced into labor on the Burma–Thailand railway endured starvation, disease, and brutality; thousands perished. These atrocities underscored how fragile international agreements were when confronted by ideological or cultural disregard for them. Japan had signed but not ratified the Geneva Convention, and its military ethos placed little emphasis on prisoner protections, seeing surrender itself as dishonorable.

By contrast, the Western Front showed a different picture. German treatment of British and American prisoners, while far from ideal, was generally more consistent with Geneva standards. Camps such as Stalag Luft III, later immortalized in

The Great Escape, operated under strict discipline but also allowed prisoners to receive Red Cross parcels, conduct educational programs, and even create theatrical productions. The Red Cross was permitted to visit, and correspondence with families, though censored, was often allowed. Mortality rates were far lower than in the East. This disparity revealed how adherence to humanitarian law could exist within the same conflict, depending on the cultural and ideological frameworks of the belligerents.

The war's end brought legal reckoning. At Nuremberg, German leaders were charged not only with crimes against peace and crimes against humanity but also with war crimes relating to prisoners. The murder and mistreatment of Soviet POWs was a central charge. The tribunal affirmed that the rules of war, including protections for prisoners, were binding even when an enemy had not signed the relevant convention. This was a crucial development: it reinforced the idea that the law of war derives not just from treaties but from custom and conscience — that its protections belong to all humanity, not only to those with diplomatic signatures.

In the Pacific, the Tokyo Trials similarly prosecuted Japanese officers for the abuse and murder of prisoners. General Homma Masaharu was executed for his role in the Bataan Death March, and others faced long prison sentences for crimes against Allied captives. These trials cemented the principle of command responsibility — that leaders could be held accountable for the actions of their subordinates if they knew, or should have known, of atrocities and failed to prevent them.

The horrors of the Second World War propelled a major legal reform. In 1949, the Third Geneva Convention was adopted, greatly expanding and clarifying the rights of prisoners of war. It mandated adequate food, shelter, and medical care, required protection from violence and intimidation, and enshrined the right of correspondence. It regulated labor, forbidding dangerous or degrading work. Perhaps most importantly, it provided detailed mechanisms for oversight, including the continued role of neutral organizations such as the Red Cross. Where earlier law had left gaps, Geneva III sought to fill them, responding directly to the lessons of the war.

The Cold War years tested these principles. In Korea, captured soldiers on both sides were subjected to political indoctrination, and allegations of brainwashing surfaced. Some prisoners refused repatriation at war's end, a shocking development that highlighted the complexity of personal choice under duress. The armistice of 1953 included supervised exchanges under international auspices, demonstrating the enduring relevance of neutral intermediaries. In Vietnam, the situation was harsher. American prisoners in North Vietnamese hands — most famously John McCain, later a U.S. senator — endured years of mistreatment and solitary confinement at the "Hanoi Hilton." The North Vietnamese government insisted they were "war criminals," not entitled to Geneva protections, a claim widely rejected by the international community. Here again, the fragility of enforcement was plain: without reciprocal leverage or robust international mechanisms, compliance with the law of war depended largely on political calculation.

The late twentieth century saw renewed efforts at enforcement through international tribunals. The International Criminal Tribunal for the former

Yugoslavia (ICTY), established in 1993, prosecuted abuses of prisoners during the Balkan conflicts. Cases such as *Prosecutor v. Delalić* (the "Čelebići case") addressed conditions in detention camps where Bosnian Serbs, Croats, and Muslims each held enemies in brutal confinement. The tribunal held that murder, torture, and cruel treatment of prisoners constituted grave breaches of the Geneva Conventions, and it convicted several camp commanders. This jurisprudence extended Nuremberg's principles into the post–Cold War world, affirming that mistreatment of prisoners was not a relic of the past but a continuing danger.

The International Criminal Tribunal for Rwanda (ICTR) also confronted prisoner-related abuses, though in the context of genocide rather than traditional warfare. In both tribunals, the principle of individual criminal responsibility was sharpened: it was no defense that one had merely followed orders. Leaders who directed or tolerated abuse of captives could face justice decades later, reinforcing deterrence for future conflicts.

Parallel developments occurred in conventional law. The Additional Protocols to the Geneva

Conventions in 1977 further strengthened protections for prisoners, extending them to conflicts of a non-international character, such as civil wars. This was significant because many late twentieth-century conflicts fell outside the traditional state-versus-state framework. The law of war was adapting to new realities, broadening its coverage to ensure that all persons captured in conflict, whether in uniform or not, would have some claim to humane treatment.

The principle of humane treatment for prisoners thus emerged from World War II not as a fragile aspiration but as a bedrock rule. It was tested in Korea, violated in Vietnam, and vindicated again in the Balkans and Rwanda. Its legacy is complex: compliance remains uneven, and violations persist in places such as Iraq, Syria, and Afghanistan. But the arc of history bends toward stronger, clearer rules, reinforced by both treaty and tribunal. The treatment of prisoners of war remains one of the clearest litmus tests of whether the law of war is being honored or betrayed.

Prisoners of War (Part 3)

As the twentieth century gave way to the twenty-first, the law of prisoners of war faced some of its most severe modern challenges. The rules codified after World War II and reaffirmed during the Cold War were tested by new forms of conflict: counterterrorism campaigns, asymmetrical wars, and occupations in fractured states. The era was marked not only by traditional battlefield captures but also by a category of detainees whose status lay in legal gray zones, pushing the Geneva framework to its limits.

Nowhere was this more evident than in the detention facility at Guantánamo Bay, Cuba. After the terrorist attacks of September 11, 2001, the United States launched a global campaign against al-Qaeda and its affiliates. When fighters were captured in Afghanistan and elsewhere, the Bush administration argued they were not entitled to prisoner-of-war protections under Geneva III, branding them "unlawful enemy combatants." This phrase was not found in the Conventions but was meant to distinguish them from both civilian criminals and lawful POWs. The rationale was that groups like al-Qaeda did not wear uniforms, did not carry arms openly, and did not conduct operations in accordance with the laws and customs of war.

This position, however, provoked fierce debate. Human rights advocates, scholars, and foreign governments argued that the Geneva Conventions apply to all armed conflicts, regardless of the adversary's identity. The International Committee of the Red Cross (ICRC), consistent in its neutral role, insisted that even unlawful combatants must be treated humanely and afforded certain minimum protections. In 2006, the United States Supreme Court in *Hamdan v. Rumsfeld* held that Common Article 3 of the Geneva Conventions — which provides basic guarantees of humane treatment in all conflicts — applied to detainees at Guantánamo. This ruling marked a critical check on executive power and reaffirmed that the floor of humanitarian law cannot be avoided, even in unconventional wars.

The wars in Iraq and Afghanistan further complicated the picture. Coalition forces captured thousands of fighters from insurgent groups who often blended into civilian populations. The central question was whether these individuals qualified as POWs or as unlawful combatants. In practice, many were detained under security provisions rather than formally classified. In Iraq, notorious episodes of abuse at Abu Ghraib prison — where photographs showed prisoners humiliated and tortured by American personnel — shocked the world. These images undermined U.S. credibility, fueled insurgency propaganda, and demonstrated once again how fragile compliance could be when discipline and oversight failed. Courts-martial convicted several low-ranking soldiers, but critics argued that accountability did not extend far enough up the chain of command.

Afghanistan posed similar problems. Detainees were often held without clear procedures for status determination. The U.S. established "Combatant Status Review Tribunals" to decide whether individuals were enemy combatants, but critics argued these lacked due process and transparency. The ICRC visited detainees, but its confidential reports highlighted persistent concerns about conditions and indefinite detention. The line between traditional prisoners of war and security detainees blurred, raising fears that Geneva's carefully crafted framework was being eroded by expediency.

At the same time, these conflicts demonstrated that the law of war had not lost all force. Formal exchanges of prisoners occurred between the U.S. and Taliban intermediaries, most notably the 2014 release of Sergeant Bowe Bergdahl in exchange for five Taliban detainees from Guantánamo. This resembled older wartime swaps and confirmed that even irregular conflicts could generate negotiations around captives. Moreover, debates within the United States — in Congress, the courts, and the press — reflected an enduring awareness that the treatment of prisoners is a measure of national integrity. The law of war remained a reference point, even when contested.

Beyond America's wars, other conflicts underscored the continuing importance of POW protections. In the Balkans during the 1990s, the ICTY prosecuted not only camp guards but also political leaders who oversaw detention policies. In Africa, civil wars in Sierra Leone, Liberia, and the Democratic Republic of Congo involved mass abductions and forced recruitment of child soldiers — blurring categories but still falling under humanitarian prohibitions. The Special Court for Sierra Leone, for instance, tried commanders for cruel treatment of captives, reinforcing that individual criminal responsibility extended to irregular fighters as well as states.

A newer dimension is the impact of technology. Drone warfare and targeted killings reduce the number of battlefield captures, raising the specter of fewer prisoners but more fatalities. Some argue this undermines the protective logic of the Geneva Conventions: it is easier politically to kill suspected combatants at a distance than to capture, classify, and safeguard them. Yet even here, the law insists that killing is not always permissible, and that when enemies are hors de combat — incapacitated, wounded, or surrendering — they must be spared. The absence of POWs is not a sign that the law is irrelevant; rather, it is a sign of its circumvention, and scholars increasingly warn against normalizing "targeted killing" as a substitute for lawful detention.

Today, the International Criminal Court (ICC) continues the jurisprudential trajectory of Nuremberg, Tokyo, and The Hague. Under the Rome Statute, the mistreatment of prisoners of war is a war crime, enforceable against leaders of both states and armed groups. Though prosecutions remain limited, the existence of a permanent tribunal is itself a deterrent signal. Military manuals in many countries continue to instruct soldiers on POW treatment, embedding these norms in training and doctrine.

What emerges from this modern history is not a simple narrative of decline. Despite Guantánamo, Abu Ghraib, and other violations, the law of war remains alive. Its very contestation in courts and legislatures proves its continued relevance. The fact that abuses are hidden or denied shows that states still feel bound by its standards, even if they fall short. And when tribunals convict perpetrators or courts remind governments of their obligations, the legacy of Geneva is renewed.

In sum, the law of prisoners of war has traveled a long path. From the selective chivalry of medieval knights, to the codifications of the nineteenth century, to the cataclysm of World War II, to Guantánamo and beyond, the principle has endured: captives must be treated as human beings, not discarded as spoils. Wars will continue, and with them, captives will be taken.

The true measure of civilization is how we treat those who can no longer fight back. That is why the law of POWs is not a relic of the past, but a living shield for the future.

CHAPTER 8

OCCUPATION LAW (PART 1: DUTIES OF THE OCCUPIER)

Few areas of the law of war are as complex, or as morally fraught, as the law of occupation. To occupy a territory means that a military force has extended its control beyond its own borders, replacing the sovereign's authority with its own. Unlike conquest, occupation is presumed to be temporary. The occupying power does not acquire sovereignty over the land; it merely holds it in trust until peace is restored. Yet this legal fiction conceals a deep tension. For the people on the ground, the occupier exercises all the functions of government, and its choices determine whether daily life resembles order or oppression.

The foundations of occupation law lie in the Hague Regulations of 1907, which remain the backbone of this field. Article 42 states that territory is considered occupied when it is "actually placed under the authority of the hostile army." Control must be effective — mere raids or skirmishes do not create an occupation. Once in place, Article 43 imposes the most basic duty: the occupier must "take all the measures in his power to restore, and ensure, as far as possible, public order and safety, while respecting, unless absolutely prevented, the laws in force in the country." This deceptively simple formula is the compass for all subsequent rules. It obliges the occupier to maintain stability but not to remake society in its own image. It must preserve the legal and institutional life of the territory, intervening only when necessary for security or to comply with international obligations.

From this starting point flow several concrete duties. First, the occupier must respect the lives and property of civilians. Article 46 of the Hague Regulations declares that "family honour and rights, the lives of persons, and private property... must be respected." Pillage is "formally forbidden." The Geneva Conventions of 1949 reinforced these protections, particularly Geneva IV, which devotes its entire framework to the protection of civilians under occupation. Deportations, forced labor, and collective punishments are strictly prohibited. Article

49 of Geneva IV states bluntly: "Individual or mass forcible transfers, as well as deportations of protected persons… are prohibited, regardless of their motive." This provision, born of the Nazi deportations of millions, is among the clearest rules in humanitarian law.

Second, the occupier has duties toward the economic and social life of the territory. It may requisition goods and services, but only proportionately and with compensation. It may levy taxes, but not beyond the amounts already in force unless necessary for administration. It must ensure food and medical supplies for the population, and if local resources prove inadequate, it must permit and facilitate relief consignments. The image of the occupier as a mere caretaker is thus embedded in the law: it wields great power, but primarily in order to sustain the civilian population, not to exploit it.

Third, the occupier must safeguard cultural property and institutions. Here, the law intersects with my own scholarly preoccupation. The 1954 Hague Convention for the Protection of Cultural Property in the Event of Armed Conflict and its Protocols impose obligations to prevent the theft, destruction, or illicit export of artworks, archives, and monuments. The looting of the Baghdad Museum in 2003, when priceless Mesopotamian artifacts were stolen amidst chaos, remains a searing reminder of what is at stake when an occupier fails in this duty. Cultural treasures are not simply relics; they are the symbols of identity for a people who may otherwise feel powerless under foreign rule.

The obligations also extend to legal and judicial institutions. The occupier may not abolish local courts, nor may it impose its own penal codes wholesale. It may, however, establish military courts for security offenses, provided that fair trial guarantees are respected. After World War II, the Allied powers wrestled with this balance in occupied Germany and Japan. They dismantled fascist institutions, prosecuted war criminals, and initiated democratic reforms, yet still maintained that these actions were consistent with humanitarian law. Critics argued that this blurred the line between occupation and transformation. The law's flexibility was stretched, but not broken, and the precedents continue to inform modern debates.

Perhaps the most sensitive duty is that regarding settlements and demographic changes. Article 49 of Geneva IV, in addition to banning deportations, also prohibits the occupier from transferring parts of its own civilian population into the occupied territory. This rule emerged directly from Nazi policies of colonization in Eastern Europe. Today, it is invoked most frequently in discussions of the Israeli settlements in the West Bank. Successive UN resolutions and advisory opinions of the International Court of Justice (ICJ) have affirmed that settlement activity violates Article 49. Israel disputes this interpretation, but the debate demonstrates how occupation law remains at the heart of modern geopolitics.

Case law has given flesh to these rules. The Nuremberg Military Tribunals, in cases such as *The Hostages Case* (1948), emphasized that reprisals against civilians in occupied territories violated both the Hague Regulations and customary law. The tribunal condemned German commanders in the Balkans for executing hostages and burning villages in response to partisan attacks. These acts, it declared, were not legitimate measures of security but unlawful terror against the population. In the decades since, tribunals from the ICTY to the ICC have reinforced that occupation does not grant carte blanche. Commanders who abuse their authority are subject to prosecution.

Modern occupations illustrate both compliance and violation. The U.S.-led occupation of Iraq after 2003 initially promised to respect Iraqi laws and institutions, but in practice the Coalition Provisional Authority (CPA) issued sweeping orders that dismantled the Ba'athist system and restructured the economy. Critics argued that this went beyond the caretaker model, amounting to illegal transformation. The looting of infrastructure, shortages of food and medicine, and failure to secure public order drew widespread condemnation. By contrast, UN-mandated missions such as those in East Timor and Kosovo, though not "occupations" in the classic sense, operated with a similar mandate to maintain order while respecting local law. They highlighted how international administration can mirror occupation law's principles, even in a different institutional framework.

What emerges is a picture of occupation law as a body of restraint: a set of rules that remind the occupier that it is not sovereign, that its power is temporary and conditional, and that its legitimacy depends on its treatment of the civilian population. This law has been violated more often than it has been obeyed. Yet its presence matters profoundly. It gives civilians a language of protest, tribunals a framework for judgment, and soldiers a manual for conduct. It does not end the pain of occupation, but it sets limits that can prevent catastrophe.

Occupation Law (Part 2: Duties of the Occupied Population)

If the occupying power bears the greater weight of responsibility, the occupied population is not without obligations of its own. The law of war does not imagine civilians as passive victims alone. It also recognizes that people living under occupation face choices, and those choices can shape the difference between hardship and calamity. Occupation law therefore balances two imperatives: preserving the right of civilians to resist illegitimate control, and imposing certain duties that keep society from collapsing into anarchy.

The starting point is again the Hague Regulations of 1907, which assume that local laws remain in force "unless absolutely prevented." This means that ordinary citizens are expected to continue obeying the civil and criminal law of their own state so long as it is not suspended or contradicted by the occupier. They must pay taxes levied under lawful authority, respect property rights, and maintain the civic structures of daily life. A baker is still a baker, a teacher still a teacher. The occupier cannot demand loyalty, but it can expect compliance with the ordinary machinery of law and order. To refuse all cooperation would paralyze the very society the law seeks to preserve.

But there is a line between cooperation and collaboration. The law draws a distinction between civilians fulfilling ordinary duties and those who actively assist the occupier in suppressing their fellow citizens or committing atrocities. The trials after World War II illustrate this tension. In occupied France, for example, the Épuration légale ("legal purge") tried thousands accused of collaborating with Nazi authorities. Some were punished for denouncing resistance members, others for profiteering from confiscated Jewish property. While not all of these cases implicated the Hague Regulations directly, they reflected the enduring expectation that civilians under occupation must not aid in criminal acts. The duty of ordinary compliance does not excuse betrayal.

The question of armed resistance is even more fraught. Under the Hague Regulations, only combatants who meet certain criteria — wearing a fixed distinctive sign, carrying arms openly, and following a chain of command — are entitled to prisoner-of-war status if captured. Civilians who spontaneously take up arms against the occupier are considered *francs-tireurs* (free shooters) and may be punished as unlawful combatants. This rule emerged during the Franco-Prussian War (1870–71), when irregular fighters harassed German troops. The Germans responded with brutal reprisals, and international law codified a harsh compromise: resistance must be organized and disciplined to be lawful. Geneva Convention III later reinforced this distinction.

Yet history shows that civilian resistance rarely conforms neatly to these legal standards. The partisans in the Balkans during World War II, the French Maquis, and countless others fought in irregular fashion. When captured, they were often executed as bandits, even though their cause was national liberation. Modern law has tried to soften this rigidity. Additional Protocol I (1977) expanded protections by recognizing that guerrilla fighters may lawfully conceal themselves among civilians so long as they carry arms openly during attacks. Still, the law imposes on the occupied population a duty not to blur the line so thoroughly that civilians as a whole become indistinguishable from combatants — for then, all civilians risk losing protection.

Another duty lies in the realm of non-violence and civil protest. The law permits civilians to voice opposition, to strike, to demonstrate, and to resist peacefully. These acts may irritate the occupier, but they are not prohibited by international law so long as they do not cross into sabotage or armed action. In fact, peaceful resistance has often proven more effective than armed struggle in maintaining moral authority. The Velvet Revolution in Czechoslovakia (1989), though not an occupation in the technical sense, demonstrated how nonviolent civilian action can overwhelm an imposed power without triggering mass bloodshed. For occupied populations, the duty is not silence, but measured resistance that avoids exposing innocents to reprisal.

The obligations of the occupied also extend to preservation of cultural heritage and property. Civilians must not engage in looting, even of the occupier's abandoned supplies. They must protect monuments and archives from destruction, as these are seen as belonging to humanity at large. The looting of archaeological treasures in occupied territories, whether in wartime Iraq or earlier in Nazi-occupied Europe, shows that civilians can be complicit as well as victims. The duty to safeguard what belongs to posterity does not vanish under the shadow of foreign rule.

Finally, there is the overarching duty of humanity toward one another. Occupied populations are often tempted to turn inward, to settle old scores under cover of chaos. Pogroms, vendettas, and opportunistic violence too often erupt when state authority collapses. The law of occupation insists that civilians must not prey upon each other. The protection they demand from the occupier they must also extend to their neighbors. After the war in Bosnia, survivors testified that betrayal by neighbors — not merely the guns of strangers — left the deepest scars. The duties of the occupied are thus as much moral as legal: to hold on to the threads of community when all else frays.

Occupation law, then, is a two-sided coin. The occupier must govern with restraint; the occupied must endure with dignity. Neither side's obligations erase the other's. Together, they sketch a vision of survival in the most unnatural of conditions — when a people live under the flag of someone else's army. The rules do not make occupation just, but they make it bearable, and they preserve the possibility of peace once the occupier departs.

CHAPTER 9

CEASEFIRES, ARMISTICES, AND THE WHITE FLAG

When a warring power "sues for peace," it means that one of the belligerent parties formally seeks to end hostilities through negotiation rather than by total victory or surrender. It is a diplomatic act, signaling a willingness to stop fighting and to explore terms of settlement. This can happen for many reasons—military exhaustion, economic collapse, outside diplomatic pressure, or recognition that further fighting will only deepen losses. Suing for peace does not necessarily mean unconditional surrender. The outcome may be an armistice (a suspension of hostilities), a peace treaty with negotiated terms, or even a partial settlement leaving some issues unresolved. What matters is that the warring power signals recognition that force alone cannot decide the conflict. This diplomatic process is as old as the practice of war itself and as modern as today's conflicts.

War does not always end in surrender. Sometimes it halts abruptly, not with a victor's flag raised but with a pause agreed to by both sides, however reluctantly. These pauses — whether brief battlefield truces, formal armistices, or ceasefires mediated by outsiders — reveal another side of the law of war: not only how to fight, but how to stop fighting, at least for a time.

The most enduring symbol of this tradition is the white flag of truce. Its roots go deep into history, though its codification came in the Hague Conventions of 1899 and 1907, which recognized the right of belligerents to parley under a flag of truce. The white flag is more than a scrap of cloth: it embodies an expectation of safety for envoys and negotiators, even when they walk across ground still smoking with gunfire. Misuse of the flag — approaching under its protection to spy, attack, or deceive — is considered perfidy, one of the gravest violations of honor in war.

Battlefield truces have long served practical needs. Even bitter enemies have recognized moments when fighting must pause: to bury the dead, collect the wounded, or negotiate prisoner exchanges. In medieval Europe, heralds under truce carried messages between kings, risking their lives but were usually respected as inviolable. The custom continued into the modern age. During the American Civil War, flags of truce were often raised to negotiate exchanges of prisoners, or simply to recover bodies from contested ground.

Sometimes these ad hoc truces emerged spontaneously from soldiers themselves. The most famous example is the Christmas Truce of 1914 during the First World War, when British and German soldiers, exhausted by weeks in the trenches, laid down their rifles and stepped into no man's land. They shared food and carols, even playing makeshift games of football. It was not commanded from above but rose from the humanity of men who recognized, however briefly, that their enemy was just as cold and weary as themselves. Military authorities quickly suppressed such truces, fearing they would undermine discipline, but the memory endures as proof that even amid industrial slaughter, the impulse toward peace flickers.

The law of war protects these fragile intervals. The Hague Conventions require that persons carrying a flag of truce be respected and protected, unless it is proven they have abused the privilege. To harm an envoy under safe conduct is not merely dishonorable; it is a war crime. Later practice, especially in the twentieth century, expanded the notion of truces to include humanitarian ceasefires — temporary pauses brokered to allow aid to reach civilians or to evacuate noncombatants from besieged areas.

Thus, woven into the fabric of the law of war is not only the management of violence, but also the recognition that violence must sometimes yield to a pause in the fight. A ceasefire is more than a tactic; it is a statement that war is not absolute, that killing can stop.

CEASEFIRES, ARMISTICES, AND THE WHITE FLAG (PART 2)

When a war grows too exhausting to continue, the law of war provides more structured instruments than the white flag or a momentary truce. These are armistices and ceasefire agreements — legally recognized pauses in hostilities that can endure for days, months, or even decades.

One of the most famous examples is the Armistice of Compiègne in November 1918. After years of attritional bloodshed, German envoys crossed into France under safe conduct to meet Allied leaders in a railway carriage in the forest of Compiègne. The agreement they signed was not a peace treaty — that would come months later in Versailles — but it silenced the guns. The armistice ordered German forces to withdraw behind the Rhine, surrender equipment, and release prisoners, while the Allies halted their advance. What mattered most to the common soldier was that the shelling finally stopped. The law of war recognizes such agreements as binding instruments; to resume hostilities without cause would be a violation of good faith and an act of treachery.

The Second World War ended differently, with outright surrenders in Berlin and aboard the USS Missouri in Tokyo Bay. But the principle of armistices lived on. In 1953, after three years of stalemated fighting in Korea, the United Nations Command, North Korea, and Chinese forces signed an armistice agreement at Panmunjom. It established the Demilitarized Zone (DMZ), supervised by neutral observers, and created a mechanism for prisoner exchanges. Crucially, no peace treaty followed — and technically, the Korean War has never formally ended. The armistice, a pause rather than a conclusion, has endured for seventy years. It is a vivid example of how cessation agreements can become semi-permanent fixtures in international relations.

Modern conflicts continue this pattern. In the Middle East, the United Nations has brokered ceasefires in Lebanon, Syria, and Gaza. These agreements often establish "humanitarian corridors" — temporary suspensions of fighting so civilians can be evacuated or aid delivered. While fragile and often violated, they show the continued relevance of the idea that war can be bracketed, even if not resolved. The law of war insists that once a ceasefire is agreed, both sides must honor it; to shell a civilian convoy during an agreed pause is not just dishonor but a war crime.

Armistices and ceasefires also underscore the law's concern for safe negotiation venues. Envoys must be protected; venues must be secure. To target or assassinate negotiators is universally condemned.

This principle, dating back to the earliest heralds and envoys, was reinforced in the Hague Conventions and survives in modern diplomatic law. When diplomats enter talks under flag of truce or UN escort, they embody the hope that words can replace weapons.

Ceasefires, Armistices, and the White Flag (Part 3)

Ceasefires and armistices are never the end in themselves. They are bridges, fragile and temporary, pointing toward what may come next. Sometimes they collapse, plunging both sides back into violence. Other times, they open the door to sustained negotiations and a new political order. The law of war, in its quiet way, underwrites this transition by providing protections for those who dare to sit down with the enemy.

The principle of safe conduct for negotiators is among the oldest in the customs of war. Ancient heralds carried emblems of their king or city to signal their protected status. To slay or detain such an envoy was to desecrate the possibility of peace itself. Modern law carries this forward: the Hague Conventions require that envoys under a flag of truce be respected, and contemporary diplomatic law builds upon this tradition. When adversaries agree to meet in neutral territory — whether in Geneva, Dayton, or Camp David — their very arrival rests upon this bedrock principle.

History is full of examples where temporary cessations gave way to durable settlements. The Dayton Accords of 1995, which ended the Bosnian War, grew out of a succession of short-lived ceasefires in the Balkans. Each failed truce nevertheless carved space for the next, until the warring factions could be brought into a U.S. Air Force base in Ohio, far from the battlefields, to negotiate in security. Similarly, the Paris Peace Talks during the Vietnam War were made possible only by agreements that negotiators would not be harmed in transit, no matter how bitter the fighting continued elsewhere.

Even when peace is elusive, ceasefires can serve humanity. Humanitarian ceasefires in Syria, Sudan, and elsewhere have permitted civilians to flee sieges, aid convoys to enter starving towns, and medical evacuations to proceed. Each instance may last only hours or days, but the law of war insists that these pauses be honored. To strike during a declared humanitarian corridor is not merely a breach of faith; it is a war crime.

The symbolism of cessation runs deep. A white flag raised on the battlefield, an envoy walking unarmed into enemy lines, a signed armistice laying down conditions for silencing of the guns — these are moments when law and humanity assert themselves against the chaos of combat. They do not erase the war, but they mark it with restraint, and sometimes, with hope.

Courtesies Between Captains at Sea

Finally, I want to cover briefly something that has fascinated me since my youth, namely the treatment of defeated commanders by the victorious commanders following a battle at sea.

From the earliest sea battles, how a victorious captain treated his defeated counterpart reflected not only the fortunes of war but also the values of the age. In the ancient Mediterranean, mercy was rare: Phoenician or Greek victors might enslave or execute enemies. Yet even then, messengers of surrender were granted safe conduct, and distinguished officers could be spared as valuable hostages. Rome, by contrast, made a grim spectacle of defeated admirals, displaying them in triumphs before consigning them to prison or death. Courtesy was an exception, not a rule.

By the seventeenth and eighteenth centuries, the sea had become the domain of professional officer corps, and the Age of Sail gave rise to a culture of honor among naval commanders. Victorious captains often invited their defeated counterparts aboard, accepted the formal surrender of a sword, and—sometimes—returned it as a gesture of respect for gallantry. Horatio Nelson himself set the tone at the Battle of the Nile (1798): though merciless in victory, he ordered humane treatment of captured French officers and ensured they were recognized as men of honor. Across maritime Europe, dinner on the victorious ship at the captain's table, and often parole, for a defeated commander, and polite conversation became part of the ritual, reinforcing that even enemies shared the burdens of command.

In modern times, these traditions became bound up with international law. During the Second World War, despite brutal total war, naval courtesies persisted. After the *Bismarck* was sunk in 1941,

British destroyers risked their own safety to rescue German survivors, including senior officers. And in 1945, aboard the USS *Missouri*, Admiral Nimitz and General MacArthur orchestrated Japan's surrender with a careful choreography of courtesy: Japanese envoys were treated with formality and respect, even as they signed away their empire. Today, under the Geneva Conventions, captured commanders are guaranteed humane treatment, but the old spirit survives in the symbolism of surrender. The defeated captain remains more than just a prisoner—he is a fellow mariner, accorded dignity in recognition of the common perils of the sea.

This chapter sits as the natural hinge between the conduct of hostilities and the governance of what follows. To pause a war, even without victory, is to acknowledge that war is not absolute, that killing has limits.

The law of war, by protecting truces, armistices, and the envoys who bear them, ensures that even amid violence, there remains always a path back to words.

CHAPTER 10

NEUTRALITY AND COLLECTIVE SECURITY (PART 1)

War is never fought in isolation. Even when two states collide, the ripple effects reach far beyond their borders, forcing other nations to decide whether to stand aside, intervene, or align themselves with one side. Neutrality and collective security represent opposite poles of this spectrum — one insisting on abstention and impartiality, the other on solidarity and joint action. Both are deeply embedded in the law of war, and both have been tested in practice, sometimes with great success and sometimes with tragic failure.

The law of neutrality emerged in the early modern period, when expanding trade networks made it essential for non-belligerents to safeguard their rights during conflicts. The Treaty of Westphalia (1648), though best remembered for ending the Thirty Years' War, also affirmed the principle that sovereign states could remain outside conflicts without forfeiting their independence. As maritime empires grew, neutrality became especially important at sea. The Armed Neutrality Leagues of the 18th century, led by Russia and joined by several northern European states, declared that neutral vessels had the right to trade freely, even with belligerents, provided they did not carry contraband. This was a direct challenge to Britain's naval dominance and its practice of intercepting neutral ships. Such disputes foreshadowed the detailed codifications that came later.

By the 19th century, neutrality had become a settled principle. The Declaration of Paris (1856), signed after the Crimean War, abolished privateering and strengthened the rights of neutral shipping. Later, the Hague Conventions of 1907 elaborated rules on the rights and duties of neutral powers, both on land and at sea. Neutral states must not allow their territory to be used for military purposes, nor can they provide troops or war materials to belligerents. At the same time, belligerents must respect neutral territory and refrain from drawing neutrals into their disputes. These rules remain part of customary law, though in practice neutrality has often been precarious.

The two world wars revealed the fragility of neutrality. In 1914, Belgium declared its neutrality, as it had been guaranteed by the great powers in 1839. Yet Germany's invasion of Belgium shattered that guarantee, drawing Britain into the war. The violation of Belgian neutrality became a rallying cry, proof that even solemn treaties could be cast aside by aggressors. In the Second World War, Switzerland maintained its neutrality through a combination of diplomacy, geography, and military preparedness, though not without controversy. Its financial dealings with Nazi Germany and restrictions on Jewish refugees remain subjects of debate. Sweden too stayed neutral, but allowed German troop transports early in the war, raising questions about the thin line between neutrality and tacit collaboration. These cases illustrate the ambiguity of neutrality when survival itself is at stake.

The 20th century also brought a new idea: that neutrality might be not only a right but a duty. The Kellogg–Briand Pact of 1928, which sought to renounce war as an instrument of national policy, was a step in this direction, though ultimately unenforceable. After the Second World War, the creation of the United Nations transformed the landscape. The UN Charter, especially Articles 39–51, established a system of collective security. The Security Council could determine threats to peace and authorize military action. Article 51 affirmed the inherent right of self-defense, but beyond that, states were expected to act together rather than remain aloof. Neutrality, in this system, was no longer sacrosanct. If the Security Council called for sanctions or force, members were bound to comply.

One of the most striking manifestations of this shift came with the North Atlantic Treaty Organization (NATO), founded in 1949 under Article 51's principle of collective self-defense. NATO created a binding commitment: an attack on one would be considered an attack on all. This went beyond mere alliance; it effectively pooled sovereignty in matters of defense. Member states agreed to subordinate their command chains to a supranational structure in certain circumstances, giving NATO the character of a warring power when engaged in operations. For the first time, an international organization acquired not only political but operational military authority. Other alliances, such as the Warsaw Pact, mirrored this structure during the Cold War, though with varying levels of autonomy for members.

The law of neutrality has adapted to this world of collective security with difficulty. Traditional neutrality, as once practiced by Switzerland or Sweden, is still possible but increasingly constrained by treaty obligations, economic interdependence, and global norms against aggression. In modern conflicts, the line between neutral and participant is blurred by sanctions, intelligence-sharing, and logistical support. Yet the principle of neutrality remains vital, offering states a legal basis for staying out of wars and a humanitarian role as intermediaries. It is no coincidence that many prisoner exchanges and peace negotiations still rely on neutral venues such as Geneva.

Neutrality and Collective Security (Part 2)

The Cold War transformed neutrality into both a shield and a burden. States caught between the U.S.-led NATO alliance and the Soviet-led Warsaw Pact were forced to navigate their neutrality carefully, lest they be absorbed into the ideological struggle.

Austria provides one of the clearest examples. In 1955, after a decade of Allied occupation, Austria declared permanent neutrality as a condition for regaining full sovereignty. This neutrality was not merely a policy but a constitutional commitment, binding Austria to avoid all military alliances and prohibit foreign bases. It allowed Austria to thrive as a mediator and host for international organizations, from OPEC to the International Atomic Energy Agency. Neutrality became Austria's identity, demonstrating how a small state could secure autonomy through law and diplomacy.

Finland's experience was more precarious. Sharing a long border with the Soviet Union, Finland signed the 1948 Treaty of Friendship, Cooperation, and Mutual Assistance, which bound it to resist Western aggression but also to remain outside NATO. This "Finlandization" became a term of art for the compromises small states make to preserve independence in the shadow of great powers. Unlike Austria, Finnish neutrality was less a voluntary posture than a survival strategy, but it nevertheless allowed Finland to maintain democracy and sovereignty while avoiding Soviet domination.

During this same era, collective security under the United Nations was tested in Korea. In 1950, the Security Council authorized a military response to North Korea's invasion of the South, marking the first large-scale UN-sanctioned war. The Soviet Union, boycotting the Council at the time, could not exercise its veto. This action revealed the potential strength of collective security, as dozens of nations contributed forces under the UN banner. Yet the Korean War also showed the limits: political deadlock soon paralyzed the Council during later crises, such as Vietnam, where neutrality was asserted by some but ignored by the great powers.

Neutrality in practice was further complicated by wars of national liberation. In Algeria, Angola, and Vietnam, revolutionary movements invoked self-determination under the UN Charter to justify armed struggle, while colonial powers often insisted that neutral states not aid insurgents. The tension between neutrality, solidarity, and the right of peoples to resist domination exposed fault lines in the legal order. The 1977 Additional Protocol I to the Geneva Conventions reflected this tension by extending combatant status to fighters in anticolonial wars, provided they observed humanitarian rules. Neutrality, in such cases, had to reckon with legitimacy claims on both sides.

The Gulf War of 1991 provided another major test of collective security. When Iraq invaded Kuwait, the Security Council authorized force to expel Saddam Hussein's army. Unlike Korea, this operation enjoyed near-universal backing, with NATO states, Arab allies, and others forming a coalition. Neutral states like Switzerland and Sweden supported sanctions but not combat, reaffirming their traditional role as providers of humanitarian relief. The war thus highlighted both poles: the binding force of collective action under the UN and the continued space for neutrality in humanitarian service.

In more recent decades, neutrality has faced new challenges. The "War on Terror," launched after the attacks of September 11, 2001, blurred the line between war and policing. Neutral states found it increasingly difficult to remain detached when global networks of terrorism, finance, and intelligence demanded cooperation. Swiss banks, for example, were pressured to freeze terrorist assets, raising the question: does economic enforcement erode neutrality? Similarly, Ireland and Austria allowed overflight rights for NATO forces in Afghanistan, prompting debate over whether such cooperation undermined their neutral status.

At the same time, collective security remains hamstrung by politics. In Syria, Security Council deadlock prevented a unified response, forcing coalitions outside the UN framework to take action. Russia's invasion of Ukraine in 2022 further tested neutrality. Switzerland, long a byword for neutrality, broke precedent by joining European Union sanctions against Moscow, declaring that neutrality could not mean indifference to aggression. This shift illustrates how neutrality, though legally protected, must constantly adapt to moral and strategic realities.

The jurisprudence of international courts has reinforced these trends. In Nicaragua v. United States (1986), the International Court of Justice condemned U.S. support for the Contra rebels as a violation of Nicaragua's sovereignty and of the duty of states to refrain from unlawful intervention. The Court reaffirmed that neutrality is not only a privilege but a duty: states must abstain from aiding belligerents in unlawful wars. This case, while ignored in practice by Washington, remains a cornerstone in the legal understanding of neutrality.

Today, neutrality and collective security coexist uneasily. Neutrality offers states a refuge and a humanitarian role, while collective security aspires to bind them to a shared system of accountability. NATO, the UN, and other alliances show that solidarity can restrain aggression, but their success depends on political will. Neutrality shows that abstention can preserve peace for some, but its survival depends on the restraint of others. Both principles, fragile though they are, continue to serve as guardrails against total war.

Neutrality and Non-International Armed Conflicts (Part 3)

The twentieth century revealed that most wars were not between states, but within them. Civil wars, insurgencies, and revolutions replaced the great interstate clashes of earlier centuries. Yet these internal conflicts were often the most brutal, because neighbors and kin turned against one another, and because the temptation to regard opponents as criminals rather than combatants was strong. The law of war could not ignore this reality; it had to adapt.

The cornerstone is Common Article 3 of the Geneva Conventions (1949). Its language is deceptively simple: in "armed conflict not of an international character," all parties — state and non-state — must treat persons humanely. The article forbids murder, torture, hostage-taking, and unfair trials. It is so fundamental that the International Court of Justice has called it a "mini-convention within the Conventions." For the first time, international law reached inside the borders of states to regulate how governments treat their own citizens in war.

This principle was tested in Rwanda (1994). The genocide against the Tutsi was not a war between states but an eruption of mass killing within one. The creation of the International Criminal Tribunal for Rwanda (ICTR) showed that even in internal conflicts, international law could prosecute crimes. Jean Kambanda, the Prime Minister of Rwanda, was convicted of genocide and sentenced to life imprisonment — the first head of government so punished. The ICTR also prosecuted media leaders who incited violence, proving that propaganda could itself be a weapon of war.

The Yugoslav wars of the 1990s gave rise to the International Criminal Tribunal for the Former Yugoslavia (ICTY), where figures like Radovan Karadžić and Ratko Mladić were convicted of genocide and crimes against humanity. Their trials reinforced that civil wars, sieges, and ethnic cleansing are subject to the same humanitarian law as conflicts between states. Slobodan Milošević, once a sitting head of state, was indicted but died before judgment — itself a reminder of the fragility of justice. The ICTY's jurisprudence, especially on unlawful targeting, command responsibility, and sexual violence, has become binding precedent far beyond the Balkans.

Another landmark was the Special Court for Sierra Leone (2002–2009), which prosecuted Charles Taylor, former President of Liberia, for aiding atrocities across the border. Taylor's conviction for crimes against humanity showed that even powerful leaders could not evade the reach of law, and that responsibility in civil wars could cross frontiers.

These tribunals also addressed the status of irregular forces and militias. Fighters in civil wars often lack uniforms or formal command structures. International law traditionally denied them prisoner-of-war status, but even Universal jurisdiction are entitled to humane treatment. In Prosecutor v. Tadić (ICTY, 1997), the tribunal clarified that non-state actors could commit war crimes in non-international conflicts. This decision shattered the old notion that only states were bound by humanitarian rules; now, every armed group, whether rebel, militia, or terrorist organization, could be held accountable.

The problem of terrorism has made these questions sharper. After the attacks of September 11, 2001, the United States declared a "War on Terror," detaining fighters at Guantánamo Bay as "unlawful enemy combatants." The U.S. position was that such individuals fell outside Geneva protections. Yet the U.S. Supreme Court, in Hamdan v. Rumsfeld (2006), ruled that Common Article 3 applies even to Al-Qaeda detainees, affirming that no armed conflict is entirely lawless. This judgment underscored the universality of humanitarian norms: they bind everyone, everywhere, regardless of labels.

Customary law has also evolved. The prohibition of torture, the ban on targeting civilians, and the rule of fair trials are recognized as jus cogens norms — peremptory rules from which no derogation is permitted. This means that even if a state has not ratified a treaty, or even if it claims "emergency," it cannot lawfully set aside these prohibitions. Torture, genocide, and deliberate targeting of civilians remain crimes, whether committed by governments or insurgents.

The jurisprudence of non-international armed conflicts reveals an important truth: law follows suffering. Rwanda, Yugoslavia, Sierra Leone — each atrocity forced the international community to reaffirm that humanity applies even in civil war. The same can be said of modern cases. In Syria, hospitals bombed by government forces and civilians starved in sieges have been condemned as violations of international law. In Yemen, starvation has been weaponized, despite clear prohibitions in Additional Protocol II. In Myanmar, the persecution of the Rohingya has been called a genocide by some states and referred to the International Court of Justice.

Each situation reminds us that the law is fragile, but not absent.

At the same time, insurgents themselves are bound by law. The recruitment of child soldiers, the use of rape as a weapon, the deliberate targeting of civilians — these acts are as unlawful for rebels as for governments. The Rome Statute of the International Criminal Court (1998) confirmed this by granting jurisdiction over crimes committed in both international and non-international conflicts. Thus, leaders of rebel groups, like the Lord's Resistance Army in Uganda, have been indicted and pursued across borders.

Non-international armed conflicts are thus no longer "domestic matters" beyond law's reach. They are part of the international order of accountability. The principle is simple, but profound: suffering knows no borders, and neither should law.

CHAPTER 11

ENFORCEMENT AND ACCOUNTABILITY (PART 1)

The law of war has always walked a narrow path between aspiration and enforcement. Rules written in treaties or declared on parchment mean little if those who violate them suffer no consequence. "Law without enforcement," one Nuremberg jurist remarked, "is only aspiration." The great test of humanitarian law, then, is whether it can hold individuals — not just states — accountable when atrocity is committed.

For most of history, war crimes were punished, if at all, by victors' justice. Ancient armies sometimes executed captured leaders after battle, not out of principle but out of vengeance. Medieval kings occasionally put defeated rivals on trial, though more often the trial was a spectacle to justify execution. There was no consistent standard, no permanent court, and no sense that humanity itself had been violated.

The first glimmer of international accountability appeared in the 15th century when Peter von Hagenbach, a Burgundian knight, was tried in 1474 by a panel of judges from the Holy Roman Empire for atrocities against civilians in Breisach. He defended himself by saying he was "just following orders," but the tribunal rejected this and convicted him. Though exceptional, this trial foreshadowed principles that would emerge centuries later: command responsibility, the invalidity of blind obedience, and the idea that crimes against civilians transcend politics.

The Napoleonic Wars saw further experiments. After Napoleon's defeat in 1815, the Allies debated putting him on trial for crimes against peace, though they ultimately exiled him to Saint Helena instead. Still, the notion that leaders might be judged for waging aggressive war had taken root.

The 20th century was the crucible in which enforcement finally became systematic. The devastation of World War I left Europe groping for justice. The Treaty of Versailles (1919) called for the prosecution of Kaiser Wilhelm II for "a supreme offense against international morality," but the

Netherlands, where he had fled, refused extradition. A handful of German officers were tried in the Leipzig Trials (1921), but sentences were light and many acquitted, revealing the weakness of enforcement without international machinery.

After World War II, however, the Allies made a different choice. At Nuremberg (1945–46), 22 major Nazi leaders were tried before an International Military Tribunal composed of judges from the United States, Britain, France, and the Soviet Union. For the first time, international law treated individuals as responsible for crimes against peace, war crimes, and crimes against humanity. Twelve were sentenced to death, three acquitted, and the rest imprisoned. Most famously, the defense of superior orders was rejected: "following orders" could mitigate but never excuse atrocity. Justice Robert Jackson, chief U.S. prosecutor, declared that "the law must reach men who possess themselves of great power and make deliberate use of it to set in motion evils which leave no home untouched."

The Tokyo Trials (1946–48) prosecuted leaders of Imperial Japan. Seven were executed, sixteen sentenced to life. These proceedings reinforced that the duty to obey humanitarian law was universal, and that aggression itself was a crime. Critics pointed out that Allied atrocities — such as the atomic bombings of Hiroshima and Nagasaki — were excluded from scrutiny, raising questions of victor's justice. Yet the precedents of Nuremberg and Tokyo established a framework that still shapes accountability today: leaders cannot hide behind state sovereignty, crimes against humanity transcend borders, and international law binds individuals.

The decades that followed showed both progress and retreat. The Eichmann trial (Jerusalem, 1961) demonstrated the principle of universal jurisdiction. Adolf Eichmann, architect of the Holocaust's deportations, was captured in Argentina, tried in Israel, convicted, and executed. The court affirmed that crimes against humanity are "not committed against one people but against humanity as a whole," and therefore any state may prosecute them.

Other efforts faltered. During the Cold War, great power rivalry paralyzed the Security Council, making international tribunals impossible. Atrocities in Biafra, Cambodia, and Afghanistan went largely unpunished at the time. Yet the memory of

Nuremberg lingered, waiting for the moment when political conditions would allow its revival.

That moment came in the 1990s, with the horrors of Rwanda and Yugoslavia. The international community, shamed by images of genocide and ethnic cleansing, created the first ad hoc criminal tribunals since Nuremberg. The ICTY (International Criminal Tribunal for the Former Yugoslavia, 1993) indicted and eventually convicted dozens of leaders for crimes ranging from unlawful targeting to genocide at Srebrenica. Radovan Karadžić and Ratko Mladić received life sentences. The ICTR (International Criminal Tribunal for Rwanda, 1994) went further, convicting Prime Minister Jean Kambanda of genocide — the first head of government found guilty by an international court. Radio broadcasters and militia leaders were also prosecuted, showing that incitement and propaganda could be criminal acts of war.

These tribunals breathed life into humanitarian law. They showed that individuals, not just states, could be called to account. They developed doctrines of command responsibility, clarified the definition of genocide, and recognized rape and sexual violence as weapons of war. Their legacy endures in the jurisprudence of the International Criminal Court.

The principle was reaffirmed in Africa when Hissène Habré, former dictator of Chad, was convicted by a special African tribunal in Dakar in 2016. He was sentenced to life imprisonment for crimes against humanity, war crimes, and torture. For the first time, an African court, supported by the African Union, tried and convicted a former head of state for atrocities committed in Africa. Victims, who had pressed for decades, finally saw justice.

These moments illustrate both the progress and fragility of enforcement. Each tribunal was born of crisis. Each depended on political will. And each showed that without enforcement, the law of war risks becoming merely "a noble aspiration," as critics sometimes put it. But with enforcement, however halting, the law becomes real: a restraint on commanders, a protection for civilians, a vindication for victims.

Enforcement and Accountability (Part 2)

The ad hoc tribunals of the 1990s set the stage for a permanent court. Out of their precedents grew the Rome Statute (1998), establishing the International Criminal Court (ICC) in The Hague. It entered into force in 2002, marking the first standing tribunal with jurisdiction to prosecute individuals for genocide, crimes against humanity, war crimes, and the crime of aggression. For many, this was the culmination of the Nuremberg promise: never again should atrocity go unanswered because politics blocked accountability.

The ICC differs from earlier efforts in two crucial ways. First, it is permanent, not convened only after a crisis. Second, it has universal jurisdictional claims, though in practice limited to states that ratify the Rome Statute or to situations referred by the UN Security Council. Its existence means that generals and presidents must at least calculate the risk of facing justice before embarking on campaigns of brutality.

Yet the ICC has faced formidable obstacles. Some major powers — including the United States, Russia, and China — have not ratified the Statute, fearing it could be used against their own troops or political leaders. African leaders have accused the Court of bias, noting that its early prosecutions focused almost exclusively on Africa. And enforcement remains its Achilles' heel: the ICC has no police force, relying on states to arrest and surrender suspects. Thus, figures like Omar al-Bashir, indicted for genocide in Darfur, traveled internationally for years without arrest because sympathetic states refused to act.

Nevertheless, the ICC has achieved significant milestones. It secured convictions against warlords such as Thomas Lubanga of the Democratic Republic of Congo, sentenced to 14 years for recruiting child soldiers, and Dominic Ongwen, a commander of the Lord's Resistance Army, convicted on 61 counts including sexual slavery and forced marriage. The Court has also expanded jurisprudence on gender-based crimes, affirming that sexual violence is not an inevitable byproduct of war but a punishable offense.

Alongside the ICC, national courts have played an increasing role under the principle of universal jurisdiction. Spain attempted to prosecute former Chilean dictator Augusto Pinochet, leading to his arrest in London in 1998. Although he was ultimately released on health grounds, the case demonstrated that retired heads of state could no longer count on safe exile. Germany and France have tried Syrian officials for torture and atrocities under universal jurisdiction statutes. These domestic efforts complement the work of international courts, reinforcing that no safe haven exists for war criminals.

Another dimension of enforcement is what scholars call the "mobilization of shame." Even when formal prosecutions are impossible, exposure and documentation can restrain atrocities. During conflicts in the Balkans and Africa, non-governmental organizations collected testimonies, photographed mass graves, and lobbied governments. Reports by Human Rights Watch, Amnesty International, and others often pressured reluctant governments to act. Naming and shaming does not always stop atrocities, but it raises costs for violators and builds a record that can later serve prosecutors.

The Security Council has occasionally reinforced accountability by referring situations to the ICC, as with Darfur (2005) and Libya (2011). Yet here politics intrudes: Syria was never referred, blocked by Russian and Chinese vetoes in the Security Council. This inconsistency highlights the fragility of enforcement mechanisms when they depend on great power consensus.

Still, the cumulative weight of these efforts has changed the calculus of war. Generals now know that their orders may be scrutinized in The Hague, that victims may testify before an international bench, and that immunity once guaranteed by office is increasingly fragile. The shadow of prosecution has become part of strategic planning. One NATO commander admitted during the Kosovo intervention that "every target list was reviewed with Nuremberg in mind."

Enforcement and accountability, then, are not merely about trials. They are about embedding restraint into decision-making, deterring atrocities by the credible threat of judgment. The ICC, domestic courts, ad hoc tribunals, and the mobilization of shame together weave a web — imperfect, porous, and often tested, but nonetheless real. It is a web that stretches from Breisach in 1474, to Nuremberg in 1945, to The Hague today. The 1474 trial in Breisach is sometimes cited as one of the earliest known examples of a judicial proceeding where the concept of "superior orders" was rejected as a defense for atrocities, paving the way for modern international law concepts.

In the end, the law of war gains force not from words alone, but from the willingness of humanity to insist that atrocity is not only immoral, not only unlawful, but punishable. This is how law becomes more than aspiration; it becomes reality, binding even upon kings and generals.

Conclusion

The Fragile Victory of Civilization

The story of the law of war is the story of humanity's stubborn insistence that even in the darkest hours, there must be light. From Hammurabi's principle of proportionality to the Geneva Conventions of the twentieth century, from Cicero's warning that "even war has its laws" to the Red Cross workers risking their lives on the battlefield, the thread is unbroken. The law of war is not a luxury, nor a relic, but a fragile victory — always contested, always violated, yet always returning to remind us that violence cannot be allowed to consume everything.

This book has traced how different civilizations, faiths, and thinkers have pressed for restraint. We have seen how the Enlightenment thinkers like Grotius argued that sovereigns themselves must obey law, and how Henri Dunant's horror at Solferino gave birth to the Red Cross. We have seen the Lieber Instructions of the American Civil War, the Hague

Conventions, and the Geneva Conventions — each born of the recognition that unrestrained war is unendurable. And we have seen how, in the modern era, the Nuremberg and Tokyo trials, the ICTY and ICTR, and the International Criminal Court have transformed ideals into enforceable accountability.

Yet we have also seen how fragile this body of law remains. It is violated every day — when civilians are targeted, when prisoners are abused, when cultural monuments are destroyed, when starvation is wielded as a weapon. The gap between the law on paper and the law in practice remains wide. And yet, even this gap proves the law's importance: for every violation, there is a charge, a protest, a reminder that something has been transgressed. Without law, there would not even be a violation to name.

The law of war thus carries two paradoxes. The first is that it regulates what should be unthinkable — war itself. The second is that it is most visible when it fails. But this should not lead us to despair. It should lead us to vigilance. For the law's endurance is itself a victory of civilization over barbarism.

What is most striking is that the protections of this law reach across the whole of humanity. They guard soldiers and civilians, the innocent and the guilty, the sick and the dying, the chaplain praying on the battlefield, the gravedigger tending the fallen, the museum holding a people's memory, the farmer harvesting in a land under occupation. They guard sovereignty and culture, family honor and human dignity. In guarding all these things, the law of war guards us against becoming less than human ourselves.

This is why the law of war matters. It matters to the civilian mother hiding her children from shells. It matters to the prisoner who clings to the hope of exchange. It matters to the commander who must balance necessity with conscience. It matters to nations who wish to be part of civilization rather than barbarism. And it matters to future generations, who inherit from us not only the ruins of conflict but the fragile thread of rules that says: even here, there are limits.

If there is a single lesson, it is this: most wars are not won, they are stopped. The law of war ensures that when the killing stops, something remains —

dignity, culture, the possibility of friendship reborn. That fragile remainder is the seed of peace. And so, flawed and fragile though it is, the law of war is one of humanity's greatest achievements. It does not end war. But it makes us remember, even in war, what it means to be human.

NOTES ON SOURCES

This book is not footnoted like a legal treatise, but it draws on a long tradition of treaties, conventions, judicial decisions, and military general orders that make up the modern law of war. The most important among them include:

- **The Hague Conventions of 1899 and 1907**, which first established rules for declarations of war, treatment of prisoners, and limitations on certain weapons.
- **The Geneva Conventions**, beginning in 1864 and revised in 1906, 1929, and 1949, with three Additional Protocols (1977, 2005). These remain the backbone of humanitarian protections in armed conflict.
- **The Lieber Instructions (General Orders No. 100, 1863)**, issued during the American Civil War, which first codified the principle of limiting military necessity with humanity.

- **The Genocide Convention of 1948**, a landmark treaty born out of the Holocaust.
- **The United Nations Charter (1945)**, especially Article 2(4), prohibiting the use of force, and Article 51, recognizing self-defense and collective security.
- **The Nuremberg and Tokyo Tribunals (1945–1948)**, which held individuals accountable for war crimes and crimes against humanity.
- **The International Criminal Tribunal for the Former Yugoslavia (ICTY, 1993–2017)** and the **International Criminal Tribunal for Rwanda (ICTR, 1994–2015)**, which expanded accountability for atrocities in our own era.
- **The Rome Statute of the International Criminal Court (1998)**, which established a permanent global court for the gravest crimes.
- Classical writers and jurists who shaped the moral and legal traditions behind these instruments, including **Cicero (1st century BCE)**, **Augustine (4th century CE)**,

Thomas Aquinas (13th century),
Francisco de Vitoria (16th century),
Alberico Gentili (16th century), and
Hugo Grotius (1625).

These instruments, together with the judicial decisions and customary practices that followed, provide the scaffolding for the law of war as presented in this book.

About the Author

Joseph Edwards (b. 1945) is a lawyer, farmer, poet, and believer living in rural middle Tennessee. He studied French language and civilization at the Université de Lyon (Diplôme 1965), earned his Juris Doctor degree at the University of Toledo College of Law (1988), and completed his Master of Laws in international and comparative law at the University of Brussels (1990).

From 1978 to 1980, he worked in Geneva for Dr. Milan Bodi, then Secretary General of the International Civil Defence Organization, gaining early insights into the humanitarian underpinnings of international law. Later, he taught the law of international organizations as a lecturer at the University of Toledo College of Law. His long-time interest in the paradox of law in war is explored extensively in this book, which is admittedly a very short introduction to the subject.

Edwards is also the author of *Sanctified* (2013), *homodeus: an introduction to the ineffable, Poems* (2024), and *The Archbishop of Appalachia: Stories and Musings from the Archdiocese* (2025).

INDEX

(TERM LIST)

A

Abraham Lincoln, 22
Abu Bakr, 18
accountability, 28, 33, 42, 74, 84, 85, 89, 94, 110, 131, 170, 175, 178, 180, 183, 185, 186, 190, 194
ad bellum, 32
Additional Protocol I (1977), 146
aerial bombardment, 83
aggression, 27, 76, 83, 89, 165, 166, 169, 170, 180, 183
Aleppo, 96
Amnesty, 185
armed conflict, 2, 5, 6, 31, 108, 171, 173, 193

B

bal tashchit, 18
battles, 53, 73, 91, 97, 157
Bodi, 2, 6, 197
bombing, 33, 34, 44, 56, 69, 82, 92, 93, 99, 108
Brussels, 1, 5, 58, 197, 203

C

cases, 32, 67, 68, 76, 103, 141, 145, 163, 168, 174, 207, 208, 223, 227, 233, 234
Ceasefire, 149, 152, 155
child soldiers, 132, 175, 184
chivalry, 46, 134
Cicero, 5, 17, 31, 78, 189, 194
Civil Defence, 2, 6, 197
civilians, 2, 6, 7, 20, 24, 26, 27, 33, 34, 36, 39, 43, 44, 48, 49, 50, 54, 56, 57, 59, 64, 65, 70, 71, 72, 74, 78, 82, 84, 88, 91, 96, 97, 105, 106, 110, 113, 138, 141, 143, 144, 146, 147, 152, 154, 156, 174, 175, 178, 182, 190, 191, 224
command responsibility, 125, 172, 178, 181
Common Article 3, 77, 130, 171, 173
conquest,, 18, 137
cultural property, 1, 5, 23, 86, 139

D

de Pauw, 58, 203
deception, 52, 209
declarations of war, 39, 193
detention, 51, 77, 127, 129, 131, 132, 133
distinction, 32, 43, 44, 45, 47, 50, 72, 74, 78, 91, 92, 95, 97, 99, 103, 106, 108, 144, 145, 210, 217, 232
Dresden, 69, 83, 92

E

Eichmann trial, 180
emblems, 155
enemy, 8, 9, 10, 11, 12, 18, 34, 36, 45, 46, 48, 49, 51, 53, 93, 94, 95, 99, 124, 129, 131, 151, 155, 157, 173, 205, 206, 207, 208, 209, 210, 211, 217, 218, 219, 221, 222, 224, 225, 226, 227, 228, 229, 230, 232, 237, 238

F

fair trial guarantees, 140
flags of truce, 151

G

Geneva Conventions (1949), 171
genocide, 27, 41, 73, 75, 76, 85, 89, 127, 171, 172, 174, 181, 183, 184
Grotius, 21, 41, 43, 118, 189, 195
Guernica, 82, 92

H

Habré, 182
Hague Conventions, 24, 25, 39, 46, 53, 58, 63, 67, 81, 96, 110, 150, 151, 155, 162, 190, 193
Hague Regulations, 39, 44, 48, 52, 64, 121, 137, 138, 141, 144, 145
Hammurabi, 15, 28, 189
Henri Dunant, 22, 36, 38, 64, 69, 82, 189
honor, 17, 19, 24, 25, 37, 38, 44, 46, 52, 55, 64, 67, 72, 118, 150, 154, 158, 191, 211, 223, 229, 232

I

ICC, 76, 89, 133, 142, 183, 184, 185, 186
ICDO, 6
ICRC, 32, 41, 82, 130, 131
indiscriminate attacks, 39, 74, 92

J

journalists, 88
jus ad bellum, 32
jus in bello, 33

K

Kant, 21
Kellogg, 26, 163
Kosovo, 33, 93, 142, 186

L

landmines, 66, 104, 105, 106, 111, 112, 113
Lieber Instructions, 22, 28, 45, 53, 81, 93, 120, 189, 193, 205
looting, 140, 142, 147

M

Mahābhārata, 16, 43
Military manuals, 134
military necessity, 1, 16, 23, 34, 51, 54, 55, 57, 91, 95, 120, 193, 206, 214, 230
mobilization of shame, 58, 185, 186, 203
monuments, 7, 60, 97, 140, 147, 190

N

NATO, 33, 42, 44, 93, 164, 165, 166, 168, 169, 170, 186
necessity, 5, 23, 24, 31, 34, 37, 43, 45, 47, 55, 56, 57, 58, 61, 71, 91, 95, 99, 108, 117, 118, 191, 207, 208, 209, 211, 220, 222, 227, 236
neutrality, 38, 161, 162, 163, 165, 166, 167, 168, 169, 170
Nuremberg, 26, 34, 40, 41, 42, 44, 50, 53, 56, 70, 72, 75, 76, 79, 83, 84, 87, 88, 124, 127, 133, 141, 177, 179, 180, 181, 183, 186, 190, 194

O

occupation, 39, 85, 86, 87, 88, 89, 137, 138, 140, 141, 142, 143, 145, 146, 147, 148, 166, 191, 205, 213

P

perfidy, 23, 42, 46, 52, 54, 93, 150, 219, 220
POWs, 50, 121, 124, 129, 130, 133, 135
Proportionality, 45, 55, 92
protection, 1, 5, 6, 7, 16, 23, 24, 26, 27, 33, 35, 38, 47, 48, 49, 51, 52, 53, 57, 60, 67, 70, 85, 88, 95, 121, 125, 138, 146, 147, 150, 182

Q

quarter, 23, 52, 53, 54, 93, 94, 222

R

ransom, 117
rape, 76, 88, 175, 181, 216, 234, 236
reconciliation, 36, 94, 109
Red Cross, 22, 25, 28, 32, 36, 38, 52, 53, 68, 82, 93, 120, 124, 125, 130, 189
refugees, 104, 163
Rome Statute, 76, 89, 133, 175, 183, 194

S

Srebrenica, 28, 181
starvation, 88, 96, 123, 174, 190
surrender, 23, 35, 46, 52, 53, 54, 61, 93, 94, 99, 109, 123, 149, 150, 153, 157, 158, 159, 184, 210, 221
symbols, 6, 52, 53, 93, 115, 140
Syria, 28, 128, 154, 156, 169, 174, 185

T

The Warrior, 8
Tokyo Tribunal, 27, 40, 84
treaties, 7, 14, 17, 23, 25, 27, 37, 38, 42, 43, 59, 63, 65, 66, 70, 71, 72, 73, 81, 84, 93, 98, 104, 105, 109, 124, 163, 177, 193
truces, 17, 150, 151, 152, 159
Tutti fratelli, 22

U

UN Charter, 164, 167
unlawful combatants, 77, 130, 145
Urban warfare, 97

V

Verdun, 24, 25
Vitoria, 20, 195

W

war crimes, 27, 40, 41, 53, 70, 76, 89, 124, 173, 177, 179, 182, 183, 194
weapons, 9, 16, 24, 35, 39, 45, 57, 59, 61, 64, 65, 67, 68, 69, 78, 81, 92, 94, 101, 103, 104, 105, 106, 107, 108, 109, 110, 112, 113, 155, 182, 193
Weapons, 58, 59, 65, 94, 101, 104, 105, 110, 112
white flag, 52, 54, 61, 93, 150, 152, 157
women and children, 211

Z

zones, 92, 129

A note on this project: I have been working on producing this book since October of 2020, off and on, although it has been swirling around in my soul for 35 years since I sat in Professor Frans de Pauw's class in Brussels and listened to him urge us to consider the mobilization of shame when law fails, as it often does. I finally reached a point where I felt compelled to get this done. Thirty-five years was enough.

I used AI extensively in research for the book, in organizational and historical aspects of producing a brief work like this, and yes, sometimes even in drafting narrative. But hear me: It is my book. I authored it. AI reduced my workload immensely. For example, the military manual governing these matters in the United States is over 1700 pages long. I prompted the AI engine to read it and give me a distillation of its contents. I believe that took less than two minutes. I instructed it to give me reports on historical and juridical events that have faded into the fog of history. It often completed the task in just a few seconds. I could go on and on, but I will say simply that there is a new technology available to writers, a technology that provides a wonderful new way to author a work like this. Lord willing I will use this technology, or maybe an even better one, for my next book of this kind. I offer no apologies, just praise for those who brought this technology to fruition. There will always be those who criticize the "shortcuts" that we are now taking. But remember, they made the same criticisms when the printing press was invented and look where we are today.

Appendix

The Lieber Instructions

Martial Law – Military Jurisdiction – Military Necessity – Retaliation

Article 1. A place, district, or country occupied by an enemy stands, in consequence of the occupation, under the martial law of the invading or occupying army, whether any proclamation declaring martial law, or any public warning to the inhabitants, has been issued or not.

Article 2. Martial law does not cease during the hostile occupation, except by special proclamation, ordered by the commander in chief, or by special mention in the treaty of peace concluding the war.

Article 3. Martial law in a hostile country consists in the suspension, by the occupying military authority, of the criminal and civil law, and of the domestic administration and government in the occupied place or territory, and in the substitution of military rule and force for the same, as well as in the dictation of general laws, as far as military necessity requires this suspension, substitution, or dictation.

Article 4. Martial law is simply military authority exercised in accordance with the laws and usages of war. Military oppression is not martial law; it is abuse of the power that the law of war confers.

Article 5. Martial law is executed in a hostile country by military force, under the direction of the commanding officer, or of the governor appointed by him. It is incumbent upon the commander of the forces to publish and enforce the orders he may deem necessary for the proper administration of the occupied territory.

Article 6. All civil and penal law shall continue to take its usual course in the enemy's places and territories under martial law, unless interrupted or stopped by order of the occupying military power; but all the functions of the hostile government, legislative, executive, or administrative, whether of a general, provincial, or local character, cease under martial law, or continue only with the sanction, or, if deemed necessary, the participation of the occupier or invader.

Article 7. Martial law extends to property, and to persons, whether they are subjects of the enemy or aliens to that government.

Article 8. Consuls, among American and European nations, are not diplomatic agents. Nevertheless, their offices and persons will be subjected to martial law in cases of urgent necessity only; their property and business are not exempt.

Article 9. The functions of ambassadors, ministers, or other diplomatic agents, accredited by neutral powers to the hostile government, cease, so far as regards the displaced government; but the conquering or occupying power usually recognizes them as temporarily accredited to itself.

Article 10. Martial law affects chiefly the police and collection of public revenue and taxes, whether imposed by the expelled government or by the invader, and whether collected in money or in kind.

Article 11. The law of war does not allow proclaiming martial law, as exercised in the sense above defined, until the commander has declared martial law, or has actually taken possession of the administrative and judicial functions.

Article 12. Whenever feasible, martial law is carried out in cases of individual offenders by military courts; but sentences of death shall be executed only with the approval of the chief executive, or of the commander of the army in the field.

Article 13. Military jurisdiction is of two kinds: first, that which is conferred and defined by statute; second, that which is derived from the common law of war. The former is exercised by courts-martial; the latter is exercised by military commissions, councils, or other tribunals.

Article 14. Military necessity, as understood by modern civilized nations, consists in the necessity of those measures which are indispensable for securing the ends of the war, and which are lawful according to the modern law and usages of war.

Article 15. Military necessity admits of all direct destruction of life or limb of armed enemies, and of other persons whose destruction is incidentally unavoidable in the armed contests of the war; it allows of the capturing of every armed enemy, and every enemy of importance to the hostile government, or of peculiar danger to the captor; it allows of all destruction of property, and obstruction of the ways and channels of traffic, travel, or communication, and of all withholding of sustenance or means of life from the enemy; of the appropriation of whatever the enemy's country affords necessary for the subsistence and safety of the army, and of such deception as does not involve the breaking of good faith either positively pledged, regarding agreements entered into during the war, or supposed by the modern law of war to exist.

Article 16. Military necessity does not admit of cruelty—that is, the infliction of suffering for the sake of suffering or for revenge, nor of maiming or wounding except in fight, nor of torture to extort confessions. It does not admit of the use of poison in any way, nor of the wanton devastation of a district.

Article 17. War is not carried on by arms alone. It is lawful to starve the hostile belligerent, armed or unarmed, so that it leads to the speedier subjection of the enemy.

Article 18. When the commander of a besieged place expels the non-combatants, in order to lessen the number of those who consume his stock of provisions, it is lawful, though an extreme measure, to drive them back, so as to hasten the surrender.

Article 19. Commanders may expel all persons not belonging to the hostile army, and not residents of the invaded district, such as traveling merchants and strangers, or subjects of neutral states, if they refuse to take the oath of allegiance to the occupying power.

Article 20. Public war is a state of armed hostility between sovereign nations or governments. It is a law and requisite of civilized existence that men live in political, continuous societies, forming organized units called states or nations, whose constituents bear, enjoy, and suffer, advance and retrograde together, in peace and in war.

Article 21. The citizen or native of a hostile country is thus an enemy, as one of the constituents of the hostile state or nation, and as such is subjected to the hardships of the war.

Article 22. Nevertheless, as civilization has advanced during the last centuries, so has likewise steadily advanced, especially in war on land, the distinction between the private individual belonging to a hostile country and the hostile country itself, with its men in arms.

Article 23. Private citizens are no longer murdered, enslaved, or carried off to distant parts, and the inoffensive individual is as little disturbed in his private relations as the commander of the hostile troops can afford to grant in the overruling demands of a vigorous war.

Article 24. The unarmed citizen is to be spared in person, property, and honor as much as the exigencies of war will admit.

Article 25. Protection of the inoffensive citizen of the hostile country is the rule; exceptions, dictated by necessity, must be rare.

Article 26. Commanders, whenever admissible, inform the enemy of their intention to bombard a place, so that the non-combatants, and especially the women and children, may be removed before the bombardment commences.

Article 27. The use of poison in any manner, be it to poison wells, or food, or arms, is wholly excluded from modern warfare.

Article 28. Retaliation will, therefore, never be resorted to as a measure of mere revenge, but only as a means of protective retribution, and, moreover, cautiously and unavoidably—that is to say, retaliation shall only be resorted to after careful inquiry into the real occurrence, and the character of the misdeeds that may demand retribution.

Article 29. Modern times are distinguished from earlier ages by the existence, at one and the same time, of many nations and great governments, related to one another in close intercourse. Peace is their normal condition; war is the exception. The ultimate object of all modern war is a renewed state of peace.

Article 30. Ever since the formation and co-existence of modern nations, and ever since wars have become great national wars, the law and usages of war have become gradually more humane, but not less energetic and effectual.

Article 31. A victorious army appropriates all public money, seizes all public movable property until further direction by its government, and sequesters, for its own benefit or that of its government, all revenues of real property belonging to the hostile government or nation. The title to such real property remains in abeyance during military occupation.

Article 32. A victorious army appropriates all public property belonging to the hostile government, such as cash, funds, and movable property. Railways, canals, telegraphs, and similar property, if they belong to the hostile government, are likewise subject to appropriation.

Article 33. It is no longer usual, as in ancient times, to enslave the population of a captured country, but the victorious army may compel the services of inhabitants in labor which does not involve taking up arms against their own country, such as repairing roads, building bridges, or carrying provisions.

Article 34. As a general rule, the property belonging to churches, hospitals, or other establishments of an exclusively charitable character is not to be seized, nor is it to be sold or confiscated, provided it is devoted to charitable purposes.

Article 35. Classical works of art, libraries, scientific collections, or precious instruments, such as astronomical telescopes, as well as hospitals, must be protected against all avoidable injury, even when they are situated in fortified places while besieged or bombarded.

Article 36. If such works of art, libraries, collections, or instruments are seized, they shall not be appropriated as booty, but they must be carefully protected and maintained for the benefit of science and the arts.

Article 37. The United States acknowledge and protect, in hostile countries occupied by them, religion and morality; strictly private property; the persons of the inhabitants, especially those of women; and the sacredness of domestic relations. Offenses to the contrary shall be rigorously punished.

Article 38. Private property, unless forfeited by crimes or offenses of the owner, can be seized only by way of military necessity, for the support or benefit of the United States army and government.

Article 39. The salaries of civil officers of the hostile government, who remain in the invaded territory and continue the work of their offices, may be appropriated to the benefit of the United States government.

Article 40. There exists no law or body of rules which authorizes the plunder and devastation of a country. Desolation and ravages are contrary to the laws and usages of modern warfare.

Article 41. All pillage or sacking, even after taking a place by main force, is prohibited.

Article 42. Slavery, complicating and confounding the ideas of property, of persons, and of war, is abolished. Enslaving populations, or forcing them into servitude, is not permitted in modern war.

Article 43. Surprising or assassinating individuals belonging to the hostile nation or army is forbidden.

Article 44. Soldiers are forbidden to kill enemies already disabled, or prisoners, and more generally, to kill enemies except in fair combat or when they cannot be secured.

Article 45. All wanton violence committed against persons in the invaded country, all destruction of property not commanded by the authorized officer, all robbery, all pillage or sacking, even after taking a place by main force, are prohibited under the penalty of death, or such other severe punishment as may seem adequate for the gravity of the offense.

Article 46. Neither officers nor soldiers are allowed to make use of their position or power in the hostile country for private gain, not even for commercial transactions otherwise legitimate.

Article 47. Crimes punishable by all penal codes, such as arson, murder, maiming, assaults, highway robbery, theft, burglary, fraud, and rape, if committed by an American soldier in a hostile country, are not only punishable as at home, but are to be regarded as aggravated by the fact that they have been committed in war, in a foreign land.

Article 48. Criminals such as highway robbers, murderers, incendiaries, poisoners, and the like, are not entitled to the privileges of prisoners of war, but shall be tried and punished as if the offense had been committed in time of peace.

Article 49. Men, or squads of men, who commit hostilities, whether by fighting, or inroads for destruction or plunder, or by raids of any kind, without commission, without being part and portion of the organized hostile army, and without sharing continuously in the war, but who do so with intermitting returns to their homes and avocations, or without a fixed military organization, are not entitled to the privileges of prisoners of war, but shall be regarded and treated as highway robbers or pirates.

Article 50. The law of nations knows of no distinction of color, and if an enemy of the United States should enslave and sell any captured persons of their army, it would be a case for the severest retaliation, if not redressed upon complaint.

Article 51. No belligerent has the right to declare that he will treat every captured man in arms of a levée en masse as a brigand or bandit.

Article 52. Men, or squads of men, who commit hostilities without being authorized by a government, or who form marauding bands to rob, plunder, or destroy, are not entitled to the privileges of prisoners of war, and shall be treated summarily as criminals.

Article 53. The enemy's chaplains, officers of the army, and civil functionaries, if captured, may be set at liberty, exchanged, or held as prisoners of war, at the discretion of the captor.

Article 54. A prisoner of war is subject to no punishment for being a public enemy, nor is any revenge wreaked upon him by the intentional infliction of suffering, or disgrace, by cruel imprisonment, want of food, mutilation, death, or any other barbarity.

Article 55. Prisoners of war are subject to confinement or imprisonment such as may be deemed necessary on account of safety, but they are to be treated with humanity.

Article 56. Prisoners of war may be released from confinement, parole excepted, at any time and returned to their country on such conditions for the benefit of the captor as may be agreed upon.

Article 57. So soon as a man is armed by a sovereign government and takes the soldier's oath of fidelity, he is a belligerent; his killing, wounding, or other warlike acts are not individual crimes or offenses.

Article 58. The law of nations allows every sovereign government to make war upon another sovereign state, and therefore the simple act of a man being a belligerent is no crime, nor does it deprive him of any of the privileges of belligerents.

Article 59. A prisoner of war remains answerable for his crimes committed against the captor's army or people before he was captured, and he may be tried and punished for such crimes.

Article 60. A prisoner of war is subject to no punishment for being a public enemy, nor is any revenge wreaked upon him by the intentional infliction of suffering, or disgrace, by cruel imprisonment, want of food, mutilation, death, or any other barbarity.

Article 61. The use of poison in any manner, be it to poison wells, or food, or arms, is wholly excluded from modern warfare. He who uses it puts himself out of the pale of the law and usages of war.

Article 62. The use of the enemy's national standard, flag, or other emblem of nationality, for the purpose of deceiving him in battle, is an act of perfidy and punishable as such. Yet, in time of war, the enemy's flag may be displayed in order to communicate with him.

Article 63. Troops who fight in the uniform of their enemies, without being ordered to do so by a commander of superior authority, and without any necessity, are guilty of perfidy, and, if captured, are punishable by death.

Article 64. The law of war does not allow proclaiming either an individual belonging to the hostile army, or a citizen, or a subject of the hostile government, an outlaw, who may be slain without trial by any captor, any more than the modern law of peace allows such intentional outlawry.

On the contrary, it abhors such outrage. The sternest retaliation should follow the murder committed in consequence of such proclamation, made by whatever authority. Civilized nations look with horror upon offers of rewards for the assassination of enemies as relapses into barbarism.

Article 65. The law of war disclaims all cruelty; all acts of torture, maiming, or wounding of defenseless individuals; all assassination or attempts at the same; all poisoning of food, drink, or wells, and all unnecessary devastation. But it does not disapprove of severity and firmness in dealing with the armed enemy, nor of measures that may secure obedience to law and restore peace.

Article 66. The law of war does not allow belligerents to force the subjects of the hostile party into the service of their own army, except in the case of volunteers.

Article 67. The law of war does not admit of the use of treachery; but it allows the employment of ruses, as well as the measure of secrecy in operations. Treachery is a violation of good faith and subjects the guilty party to punishment.

Article 68. The law of war does not admit of declaring a prisoner of war or a subject of the hostile government to be an outlaw who may be slain without trial.

The killing of prisoners of war is murder and punishable as such, unless it be in battle when they resist or when, after having been ordered to surrender, they refuse to do so.

Article 69. The law of war permits all destruction of property belonging to the enemy, which, by being destroyed, weakens him in the conduct of the war.

The destruction of property for revenge or in spite, or for any purpose not connected with the public object of the war, is forbidden.

Article 70. The law of war allows belligerents to cut off every resource of the enemy. Hence it is lawful to starve him into submission, but it is not lawful to declare that the commander will neither give quarter nor live by the usages of civilized warfare.

Article 71. The law of war does not allow proclaiming "no quarter" in a battle.

A commander is permitted to direct his troops to give no quarter in great straits, when his own salvation or that of his army absolutely requires it. But humanity, as well as the law of war, imposes upon him the duty of limiting such severity to the measure of necessity, and of treating the enemy, who is disabled by wounds or sickness, with humanity.

Article 72. Money and other private property on the person of the captured enemy, such as watches or jewelry, is regarded by modern usage as belonging to the individual prisoner, and the appropriation of the same is considered dishonorable and is prohibited.

Article 73. All prisoners of war are to be treated with humanity. Public opinion is severe upon any government that disregards this rule. The law of war does not allow any abuse of prisoners of war, nor their intentional exposure to the infectious diseases prevalent in the locality.

Article 74. Prisoners of war are subject to confinement, but they are to be subjected to no other intentional suffering or indignity. Confinement may be imposed to prevent escape, but not for revenge.

Article 75. Prisoners of war may be released on parole, if the laws of their country allow, and if they personally consent. In such cases, they are bound on their honor, and by the laws of their country, not to serve again during the war unless specially exchanged.

Article 76. A prisoner of war who has given his parole of honor and who is recaptured bearing arms against the government to which he had pledged his faith, or against the allies of that government, forfeits his right to be treated as a prisoner, and may be punished with death.

Article 77. A prisoner of war cannot be forced into the service of the hostile government, and any attempt to do so is forbidden by the law of war.

Article 78. Prisoners of war are liable to punishment for offenses committed after their capture, just as civilians are.

They may be tried and punished for crimes committed before capture, but only by the government of the place where the crime was committed.

Article 79. Every captured wounded enemy shall be medically treated, according to the ability of the medical staff.

Article 80. Honorable men, when captured, will abstain from giving to the enemy any information concerning their own army, and dishonorable acts on the part of a prisoner, especially if injurious to his own army, deprive the prisoner of the privileges of the prisoner of war.

Article 81. Partisans are soldiers armed and wearing the uniform of their army, but belonging to a corps which acts detached from the main body, for the purpose of making inroads into the territory occupied by the enemy.

If captured, they are entitled to all the privileges of prisoners of war.

Article 82. Men, or squads of men, who commit hostilities, whether by fighting or inroads for destruction or plunder, without being part of the organized hostile army, and without sharing continuously in the war, but who do so with intermitting returns to their homes, and avocations, or without being enrolled and without a uniform, are not entitled to the privileges of prisoners of war, but are to be treated as highway robbers or pirates.

Article 83. Scouts or single soldiers, if disguised in the dress of the country, or in the uniform of the army hostile to their own, employed in obtaining information, if found within or lurking about the lines of the captor, are treated as spies and suffer death.

Article 84. Armed prowlers, by whatever names they may be called, who steal within the lines of the hostile army for the purpose of robbing, killing, or of destroying bridges, roads, or canals, or of robbing or destroying the mail, or of cutting the telegraph wires, are not entitled to the privileges of the prisoner of war, and may be punished with death.

Article 85. War-rebels are persons within an occupied territory who rise in arms against the occupying or conquering army or against the authorities established by the same.

If captured, they may suffer death, whether they rise singly or in small or large bands, and whether called upon to do so by their own, but expelled, government or not.

Article 86. The law of war disclaims all cruelty and bad faith concerning engagements concluded with the enemy during the war.

Such engagements are valid, so far as the commander has the right to conclude them.

They must be observed in good faith.

But if the government disapproves of the engagement, and refuses to carry it out, the commander who made it must, so far as in his power, restore the situation to what it was before the engagement was made.

Article 87. It is a serious breach of the law of war to compel the subjects of the enemy to take part in the operations of war directed against their own country. It is contrary to the law of war to use them to point out and serve as guides.

Article 88. The law of war forbids forcing the subjects of the hostile party into the ranks of its army, and compelling them to serve against their own country.

Article 89. The law of war does not recognize the infliction of corporal punishment upon prisoners of war for disobedience of regulations. Prisoners of war cannot be confined in dungeons, nor chained, nor bound with irons, except in cases of urgent necessity.

Article 90. A spy is a person who secretly, in disguise or under false pretenses, seeks information with the intention of communicating it to the enemy.

The spy is punishable with death by hanging by the neck, whether he be a citizen of the hostile country or a stranger, and whether he belong to the hostile army or not.

Article 91. The law of war can no more wholly dispense with retaliation than can the law of nations, of which it is a branch. Yet civilized nations acknowledge retaliation as the sternest feature of war. A reckless enemy often leaves to his opponent no other means of securing himself against the repetition of barbarous outrage.

Article 92. Retaliation shall, however, only be resorted to after careful inquiry into the real occurrence, and the character of the misdeeds that may demand retribution.

Article 93. Retaliation will never be resorted to as a measure of mere revenge, but only as a means of protective retribution, and moreover cautiously and unavoidably.

Article 94. Retaliation will never be executed on the innocent, but only on the guilty, and with the utmost moderation possible under the circumstances.

Article 95. Prisoners of war are subject to no punishment for being such, but they may be punished if guilty of other crimes or misconduct.

Article 96. If prisoners of war escape and are retaken, they may be punished by confinement or stricter treatment, but not by death, unless they kill in flight, or are recaptured armed.

Article 97. Every captured wounded enemy shall be medically treated according to the ability and resources of the medical staff.

Article 98. A prisoner of war is subject to the laws and regulations of the army in whose hands he is.

Article 99. No prisoner of war can be forced to take up arms against his own country, nor to fight against its allies, nor to act as a spy against them.

Article 100. A prisoner of war who is paroled by the commander of a capturing army is bound in honor not to serve again during the war, unless exchanged.

Article 101. If the government does not approve of the parole, the paroled prisoner must return into captivity.

Article 102. A prisoner of war who breaks his parole is punishable with death.

Article 103. A prisoner of war who, after having been exchanged, is captured again, is not subject to punishment for breaking parole, but may be confined more strictly.

Article 104. The enemy's chaplains, medical officers, apothecaries, and hospital nurses are not prisoners of war, unless detained for special reasons, but they may be retained to attend their sick and wounded.

Article 105. The law of war disclaims all cruelty: no revenge, or fines, or punishments beyond what military necessity requires, shall be inflicted.

Article 106. Exchanges of prisoners take place, number for number, rank for rank, wounded for wounded. Conditions of exchange must be strictly observed.

Article 107. A prisoner of war is released by exchange or by the conclusion of peace.

Article 108. The commander of the captor has the right to release prisoners of war on parole, and the government may disapprove the agreement and order the return of the paroled soldier into captivity.

Article 109. The law of war allows every belligerent to make prisoners of war, who may be detained until exchanged or released.

Article 110. The law of war permits a commander to punish, even with death, any prisoner who, while in confinement, plots to escape or commits violence.

Article 111. All prisoners of war are liable to the infliction of retaliatory measures.

Article 112. The law of war imposes upon the detaining government the duty of providing prisoners with sufficient food, shelter, and clothing.

Article 113. The law of war requires that prisoners of war shall not be treated with cruelty, nor subjected to unnecessary suffering or indignities.

Article 114. The commander of the captor must keep exact rolls of prisoners of war, specifying names, rank, and regiment, to be furnished to the government.

Article 115. Prisoners of war may be employed in labor according to their rank and condition, and consistent with their health and strength.

Article 116. The labor of prisoners of war must not be excessive, nor should it be connected with military operations against their country.

Article 117. The government is bound to compensate prisoners of war for labor performed, according to their rank and condition.

Article 118. Prisoners of war must be treated as soldiers of honor, and must not be exposed to disgrace or insult.

Article 119. Prisoners of war must be given the liberty to correspond with their relatives, subject to reasonable restrictions.

Article 120. When officers are captured, their side arms are exempted from seizure, and they retain personal property not used for hostile purposes.

Article 121. The law of nations knows of no distinction of color, and if an enemy of the United States should enslave and sell any captured persons of their army, it would be a case for the severest retaliation.

Article 122. If the enemy shall sell or enslave any captured persons of the United States army, it shall be the duty of the United States to retaliate by the infliction of like punishment upon an equal number of captured persons of the enemy.

Article 123. The United States acknowledge and protect, in hostile countries occupied by them, religion and morality; strictly private property; the persons of the inhabitants, especially those of women; and the sacredness of domestic relations. Offenses to the contrary shall be rigorously punished.

Article 124. Offenses such as robbery, theft, burglary, fraud, forgery, embezzlement, and similar crimes, committed by members of the army against inhabitants of hostile countries, are not only punishable as at home, but in aggravated cases may be punished with death.

Article 125. Commanding officers must punish, or deliver over to the civil authorities, individuals in the service who commit such offenses.

Article 126. Neither officers nor soldiers are allowed to make use of their position or power in the hostile country for private gain.

Article 127. Crimes punishable by all penal codes, such as arson, murder, maiming, assaults, highway robbery, theft, burglary, fraud, forgery, and rape, if committed by an American soldier in a hostile country against its inhabitants, are not only punishable as at home, but in aggravated cases may be punished with death.

Article 128. The law of war disclaims all cruelty: no revenge, no maiming, no torture, no infliction of suffering for the sake of suffering.

Article 129. Retaliation is limited to the infliction of suffering for the purpose of prevention of barbarous outrages.

Article 130. The United States acknowledge and protect, in hostile countries occupied by them, religion and morality, strictly private property, the persons of the inhabitants, especially those of women, and the sacredness of domestic relations.

Article 131. The United States, however, may levy military contributions in money or kind for the support of the army, and for other military purposes.

Article 132. The United States may compel the inhabitants of hostile territory to furnish provisions and services needed by the army, but without involving them in the operations of war against their own country.

Article 133. Contributions and services shall not be imposed for the private benefit of individuals in the army, but only for the army and the government.

Article 134. As a general rule, contributions are levied in money, but if the inhabitants prefer to furnish supplies in kind, the choice is allowed.

Article 135. Officers charged with levying contributions must be duly authorized, and must account strictly for every contribution received.

Article 136. Contributions and requisitions must be proportioned as equitably as possible to the resources of the country.

Article 137. The United States acknowledge and protect hospitals, churches, places of learning, museums, scientific collections, and classical works of art, so far as possible, against all avoidable injury.

Article 138. The wanton destruction of towns, villages, or districts, the devastation of cultivated fields, and the indiscriminate slaughter of the inhabitants, are prohibited.

Article 139. The killing of prisoners, the violation of women, the killing of children, or the destruction of works of art, libraries, and scientific collections, is prohibited.

Article 140. Retaliation, however, may extend to the infliction of severe punishment for the purpose of prevention.

Article 141. Military necessity admits of all direct destruction of life or limb of armed enemies, and of other persons whose destruction is incidentally unavoidable in the armed contests of the war.

Article 142. All destruction of property not commanded by the authorized officer, all robbery, all pillage or sacking, even after taking a place by main force, all rape, wounding, maiming, or killing of such inhabitants, are prohibited under the penalty of death or such other severe punishment as may seem adequate.

Article 143. Neither officers nor soldiers are allowed to make use of their position or power in the hostile country for private gain, not even for legitimate commercial transactions.

Article 144. The law of war can no more wholly dispense with retaliation than can the law of nations. Retaliation will never be resorted to as a measure of revenge, but only as a means of protective retribution, and with the utmost moderation.

Article 145. The wanton or unnecessary destruction of a district, town, or village, is prohibited.

Article 146. The law of war does not allow proclaiming either an individual belonging to the hostile army, or a citizen, an outlaw who may be slain without trial by any captor.

Article 147. Men, or squads of men, who commit hostilities without being part of the organized army, and without sharing continuously in the war, are not entitled to the privileges of prisoners of war, but shall be treated as criminals.

Article 148. Armed prowlers, persons of the enemy's territory, who steal within the lines of the hostile army for the purpose of robbing, killing, or destroying, are not entitled to the privileges of the prisoner of war, and shall be treated as criminals.

Article 149. Scouts, or single soldiers, if disguised in the dress of the country or in the uniform of the army hostile to their own, employed in obtaining information, if found within or lurking about the lines, are treated as spies and suffer death.

Article 150. War rebels are persons within an occupied territory who rise in arms against the occupying or conquering army. If captured, they may suffer death, whether they rise singly or in bands.

Article 151. Whoever intentionally inflicts additional wounds on an enemy already wholly disabled, or kills such an enemy, is guilty of murder.

Article 152. Whoever orders or encourages soldiers to wound or kill disabled enemies shall suffer death.

Article 153. Whoever intentionally inflicts suffering on prisoners, or subjects them to cruel treatment, is guilty of a crime and shall be punished.

Article 154. The law of war forbids the infliction of suffering for the sake of suffering or for revenge.

Article 155. The law of war allows every belligerent to make prisoners of war, who may be detained until exchanged or released.

Article 156. The law of war imposes upon the detaining government the duty of providing prisoners with sufficient food, shelter, and clothing, and of treating them with humanity.

Article 157. The law of war requires that rolls of prisoners of war shall be kept, specifying their names, rank, and regiment, and that the government be informed.

Made in the USA
Monee, IL
08 November 2026

67377457R00146